IT'S A WONDERFUL LIFE

THE OFFICIAL BAILEY FAMILY COOKBOOK

IT'S A WONDERFUL LIFE

THE OFFICIAL BAILEY FAMILY COOKBOOK

INSIGHT
EDITIONS

San Rafael · Los Angeles · London

CONTENTS

INTRODUCTION

When George Bailey goes tearing through the snowy streets of Bedford Falls on Christmas Eve near the end of Frank Capra's classic film, *It's a Wonderful Life*, shouting "Merry Christmas!" to everyone he sees, the central theme of the film is distilled: Your life matters. Love is all that matters. And no matter how hard life can be, it's well worth living. Since its release in 1946, millions of people around the world have embraced this universal story about the human condition—and made watching it a beloved holiday tradition. This book celebrates the 75th anniversary of the release of the film, and its message, with recipes, crafts, and ideas for gathering you and yours around the television to take in *It's a Wonderful Life* one more time—and around the table to celebrate the shared story of all of us. As Clarence put it in the inscription he wrote in a copy of *The Adventures of Tom Sawyer* that he left for George under the Bailey family Christmas tree: "Dear George: Remember, no man is a failure who has friends."

APPETIZERS

PASTRY SNAILS 11

SWEET AND SOUR CAPONATA 13

DATE BARS 15

BLINI WITH CAVIAR 17

SPICY COCKTAIL MEATBALLS WITH YOGURT SAUCE 19

"HE'S BATS" MINESTRONE 21

PASTRY SNAILS

A Bailey family homage to a classic canapé, this recipe for flaky, cheese-filled pastry wheels is certainly a hit among all who visit Mary and George in the old Granville house.

YIELD: 8 TO 10 SERVINGS	ACTIVE: 20 MINUTES	TOTAL: 55 MINUTES

3 ounces cream cheese

3 ounces Roquefort cheese, crumbled

1 sheet puff pastry (11-by-14 inches)

½ cup finely chopped pecans

Let the cheeses stand at room temperature for 15 minutes. Meanwhile, preheat the oven to 400°F. Line two large baking sheets with parchment paper.

Roll puff pastry into a rectangle ¼ inch thick; cut in half lengthwise. In a small bowl, stir together the cream cheese and Roquefort until spreadable. For each rectangle, spread half the cheese mixture evenly over pastry; sprinkle with half the nuts. Roll up rectangle starting from one long side; pinch seam to seal. Place the spirals on a baking sheet, and refrigerate for 10 minutes.

Using a sharp knife, cut each roll into ½-inch-thick slices. Place the slices on the prepared baking sheets 1 inch apart. Bake just until golden, 12 to 15 minutes. Cool for 10 minutes before serving.

SWEET AND SOUR CAPONATA

This traditional Sicilian relish of roasted eggplant, tomato, onion, and celery—a regular addition to the table in the Martini home—gets sweetness from golden raisins, sourness from red wine vinegar, and piquancy from green olives and capers. Served on toasted Italian bread, it's lovely with a glass of chilled white wine.

YIELD: 6 TO 8 SERVINGS	ACTIVE: 25 MINUTES	TOTAL: 1 HOUR + STANDING

1 large eggplant (about 1½ pounds), cut into 1-inch cubes

4 tablespoons olive oil

Kosher salt

Freshly ground black pepper

½ cup thinly sliced yellow onion

2 stalks celery, cut lengthwise and chopped

1 cup crushed tomatoes

¼ cup golden raisins

¼ cup coarsely chopped pitted green olives

3 tablespoons red wine vinegar

2 tablespoons drained capers

2 tablespoons chopped fresh flat-leaf parsley, for garnishing

Italian bread, sliced and toasted

Preheat the oven to 425°F. On a large rimmed baking sheet, toss the eggplant with 2 tablespoons oil. Season with salt and pepper to taste. Arrange the eggplant in a single layer in the pan. Roast until eggplant is browned and tender, turning pieces halfway through roasting, about 25 minutes.

Meanwhile, in a large skillet over medium heat, add the remaining 2 tablespoons oil, plus the onion and celery. Cook, stirring occasionally, until onion is softened, 5 to 7 minutes. Add the tomatoes, raisins, olives, vinegar, and capers; stir to combine. Reduce heat to low; simmer for 10 minutes. Stir the roasted eggplant into the onion mixture. Cook over low heat until heated through, 2 to 3 minutes.

Let the caponata sit at room temperature for 1 hour to blend flavors. Sprinkle with parsley. Serve at room temperature with bread.

Tip: The caponata can be made 1 day ahead and refrigerated in an airtight container. Bring to room temperature before serving.

DATE BARS

If George Bailey had ever gotten the chance to sticker that sturdy travel case Mr. Gower gifts him with labels from Italy and Baghdad, he might have tasted the world's best dates in Iraq. As it turns out, his life is better for staying put in Bedford Falls, but he doesn't know that yet. Cut these into one-bite bars—they're just perfect for an appetizer spread.

YIELD: 24 APPETIZER-SIZE BARS	ACTIVE: 20 MINUTES	TOTAL: 1 HOUR 20 MINUTES

Nonstick cooking spray

1½ cups water

1½ cups chopped pitted Medjool dates

1 teaspoon vanilla extract

1½ cups all-purpose flour

¾ cup packed brown sugar

1 cup old-fashioned oats

1 teaspoon ground cinnamon

½ teaspoon baking soda

½ teaspoon salt

10 tablespoons unsalted butter, diced, at room temperature

Preheat the oven to 350°F. Spray an 8-by-8-inch baking pan. For the filling, in a medium saucepan, bring water to a boil over medium-high heat. Add dates; reduce heat and simmer until dates are very soft and mixture is thick and syrupy, stirring occasionally, about 10 minutes. Let cool to room temperature, about 30 minutes. Stir in vanilla.

In a large bowl, stir together the flour, sugar, oats, cinnamon, baking soda, and salt. Add the butter; blend until the mixture is crumbly. Press half the oat mixture over the bottom of the prepared pan. Spread the date filling over the oat mixture. Sprinkle with remaining oat mixture; lightly press into the filling.

Bake until golden brown and set in the center, 30 to 40 minutes. Cool completely on a wire rack. Cut into 24 bars.

BLINI WITH CAVIAR

George has big honeymoon plans: "Shoot the works. A whole week in New York. A whole week in Bermuda. The highest hotels. The oldest champagne. The richest caviar. The hottest music." A run on the bank gets in the way of all that, but there are other ways to indulge. For now, this classic Russian appetizer of bite-size buckwheat crepes topped with crème fraîche and caviar will have to do.

YIELD: 6 TO 8 SERVINGS	ACTIVE: 30 MINUTES	TOTAL: 30 MINUTES + RISING

1 cup all-purpose flour

½ cup buckwheat flour

1 teaspoon active dry yeast

1 teaspoon salt

1¼ cups whole milk

2 large eggs, lightly beaten

3 tablespoons unsalted butter, melted

Nonstick cooking spray

Crème fraîche or sour cream

Fresh dill

Caviar

In a medium bowl, whisk together the flours, yeast, and salt. Set aside.

In a small saucepan, heat the milk to 115°F to 120°F. In a small bowl, whisk together the warm milk, eggs, and butter. Add the milk mixture to the flour mixture; whisk until smooth. Cover the bowl with plastic wrap, and set in a warm place to rise for 1 hour.

Spray a medium skillet with cooking spray, and place over medium heat. Pour the batter by tablespoonfuls onto the hot skillet, and cook until golden brown on both sides, 2 to 3 minutes. Transfer the blini to a wire rack. Repeat with the remaining batter.

In a small bowl, stir together the crème fraîche and dill. Top the blini with some of the crème fraîche mixture then caviar. Serve the blini slightly warm or at room temperature.

Blini with Crème Fraîche and Smoked Trout: Top the blini with crème fraîche then thinly sliced smoked salmon or trout, and sprinkle with finely chopped chives.

Blini with Beets and Chicken: Top the blini with diced pickled beets, shredded chicken, and lemon zest.

SPICY COCKTAIL MEATBALLS WITH YOGURT SAUCE

If George had made it to Samarkand, an ancient city in Uzbekistan along the Silk Road, he might have sampled these flavorful beef or lamb meatballs served with adjika—*a spicy sauce of red chiles, tomatoes, fresh herbs, and garlic. The adjika provides the heat, while yogurt swirled with pomegranate syrup cools things down.*

YIELD: 30 MEATBALLS	ACTIVE: 50 MINUTES	TOTAL: 1 HOUR 25 MINUTES

FOR THE ADJIKA:
4 fresh red chiles
3 medium-size tomatoes, seeded
1 red bell pepper, seeded and
 coarsely chopped
1 cup lightly packed fresh cilantro
1 cup lightly packed fresh basil
 leaves
1 cup fresh dill sprigs
3 tablespoons red wine vinegar
2 tablespoons olive oil
2 tablespoons walnut oil
4 cloves garlic, coarsely chopped
1 teaspoon kosher salt

FOR THE POMEGRANATE
YOGURT SAUCE:
1 cup pomegranate juice
1 cup plain Greek yogurt
Pomegranate seeds (optional)

FOR THE MEATBALLS:
1 slice white bread, crust removed
¼ cup milk
1 small onion, finely chopped
 (½ cup)
2 cloves garlic, minced
2 teaspoons ground sumac
1 teaspoon kosher salt
½ teaspoon ground coriander
½ teaspoon freshly ground black
 pepper
¼ teaspoon cayenne pepper
1 pound ground beef or lamb

To make the adjika, remove the seeds from three of the chiles. In a food processor, combine all the chiles and remaining ingredients. Pulse until mixture forms a coarse paste. Transfer to a serving bowl, and cover until serving to let flavors blend.

To start the yogurt sauce, in a heavy small saucepan, bring the pomegranate juice to a boil over medium heat until reduced to 2 tablespoons, 5 to 8 minutes. Cover and set aside.

Preheat oven to 350°F. Line a large rimmed baking sheet with foil.

To make the meatballs, place the bread in a small bowl; pour the milk over the bread, and let stand for 5 minutes. Cut or tear the bread into pieces, reserving the milk. In a large bowl, stir together the bread pieces and milk, onion, garlic, sumac, salt, coriander, black pepper, and cayenne pepper. Add the ground beef, and gently mix until well combined. Shape the mixture into 1-inch meatballs, and place on the prepared baking sheet.

Bake the meatballs until a meat thermometer registers 160°F, about 25 minutes. Transfer the meatballs to serving platter.

To finish the sauce, spoon the yogurt into a serving bowl; drizzle with the pomegranate syrup and gently swirl. If desired, sprinkle with pomegranate seeds.

Serve the meatballs with adjika and pomegranate yogurt sauce.

"HE'S BATS" MINESTRONE

When Clarence takes George on a tour of Pottersville and the town is a crumbling den of iniquity in which no one recognizes him, George becomes understandably agitated. He catches Ernie's cab to what he remembers as his home—the "drafty old house"—that is as ramshackle and empty as it was when Mary threw a rock through the window. His agitation leads Ernie to proclaim to Bert the cop that "he's bats!" Finding neither Mary nor his children, George turns to despair. If you're ever feeling a bit on edge, stir up a pot of this soup. Each serving is topped with a bat-shaped crouton, in a nod to the night that never actually was.

YIELD: 8 SERVINGS (1 CUP EACH)	ACTIVE: 25 MINUTES	TOTAL: 50 MINUTES

2 tablespoons olive oil

1 medium yellow onion, chopped (¾ cup)

2 medium carrots, peeled and diced (1 cup)

3 stalks celery, chopped (¾ cup)

1 medium zucchini, chopped (1½ cups)

2 cloves garlic, minced

One 2-by-3-inch Parmesan rind

4 cups low-sodium vegetable broth or low-sodium chicken broth

One 14.5-ounce can diced tomatoes

One 14-ounce can crushed tomatoes

One 15-ounce can white beans, such as cannellini or great Northern, drained and rinsed

4 slices pumpernickel, wheat, or whole-grain bread, crusts removed

3 tablespoons unsalted butter, melted, or olive oil

2 tablespoons grated Parmesan cheese

2 cups fresh baby spinach or baby kale

1 teaspoon fresh lemon juice

1 teaspoon dried oregano

1 teaspoon dried basil

Kosher salt (optional)

In a stockpot or Dutch oven, heat the oil over medium. Add the onion and carrot; cook until softened, about 3 minutes. Add celery, zucchini, and garlic; cook until softened, about 2 minutes. Add the Parmesan rind, broth, tomatoes, and beans. Stir to combine and bring to a boil over medium-high heat. Reduce the heat to medium-low, and simmer until the vegetables are tender, about 15 minutes. Remove and discard the Parmesan rind.

Meanwhile, for the bat croutons, preheat the oven to 275°F. Use a small bat-shape cutter to cut eight shapes from the trimmed bread. Place the cut-outs on a large baking sheet; brush both sides with melted butter or olive oil. Bake for 5 minutes. Turn the bread over, and sprinkle with Parmesan cheese. Bake until golden and crisp, 5 to 10 minutes. Transfer to a wire rack to cool.

Return to the soup and stir in the spinach, lemon juice, oregano, and basil. Season to taste with salt if needed. Simmer until the spinach is wilted. Top servings of soup with a bat crouton.

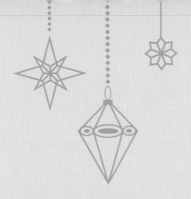

SIDES

WEDGE SALAD 25

HOME BLESSING SALAD 27

WALDORF SALAD 28

ROASTED GARLIC MASHED POTATOES 29

ROASTED KOHLRABI WITH BROWN BUTTER 31

CORN MUFFINS 33

DEVILED EGGS 34

MACARONI AND CHEESE 35

CHESTNUT DRESSING 37

CANDIED YAMS 39

HERBED TURKEY GRAVY 40

APPLE-CRANBERRY SAUCE 41

WEDGE SALAD

Annie serves up salads at family dinner just as Harry heads out to a post-graduation high school dance. There's no question this crisp and classic American salad will be a hit with anyone you serve it to. It's particularly good with steak, meatloaf, or roast beef.

YIELD: 4 SERVINGS | ACTIVE: 15 MINUTES | TOTAL: 25 MINUTES

FOR THE BLUE CHEESE DRESSING:

½ cup buttermilk

½ cup mayonnaise

1 tablespoon fresh lemon juice

½ teaspoon kosher salt

¼ teaspoon Worcestershire sauce

4 ounces firm, good-quality blue cheese, such as Roquefort, plus more for serving

¼ teaspoon freshly ground black pepper

FOR THE SALAD:

1 head iceberg lettuce, outer leaves removed

4 slices bacon, crisp-cooked and crumbled

1 cup cherry tomatoes, halved

1 tablespoon chopped fresh chives

To make the dressing, in a food processor, combine the buttermilk, mayonnaise, lemon juice, salt, and Worcestershire sauce. Process until smooth. Add the blue cheese and pulse until cheese is incorporated but still slightly chunky. Transfer to a bowl, and stir in the black pepper.

To make the salad, cut the head of lettuce into four wedges, then cut out the core. Place wedges on salad plates. Top with some of the dressing, bacon, tomatoes, and chives. Sprinkle with additional blue cheese.

HOME BLESSING SALAD

Mary blesses the Martini home with the words "bread, that this house may never know hunger." May your family always have bread on the table—and perhaps panzanella, *a traditional Italian bread and tomato salad meant to cleverly and deliciously use up stale bread (though fresh bread would do just fine). Bread cubes tossed in olive oil and toasted in the oven take on a nice crisp edge, so they hold their shape even when tossed with juicy ripe tomatoes—certainly something the Martini family will plant in the garden of their new home.*

YIELD: 8 SERVINGS	ACTIVE: 15 MINUTES	TOTAL: 55 MINUTES

¾ pound ciabatta or rustic bread, cut into 1½-inch cubes (about 6 cups)

½ cup plus 3 tablespoons extra-virgin olive oil

3 tablespoons white wine vinegar

1 clove garlic, minced

½ teaspoon Dijon mustard

½ teaspoon kosher salt

¼ teaspoon freshly ground black pepper

2½ pounds ripe tomatoes, chopped

1 cucumber, seeded, halved, and sliced

½ cup lightly packed fresh basil leaves, roughly chopped

½ small red onion, thinly sliced

3 tablespoons drained capers

Preheat the oven to 375°F. Adjust the rack to the center position.

In a large bowl, toss bread cubes with 3 tablespoons of the olive oil. Transfer to a rimmed baking sheet. Bake until golden and crisp, stirring once, 10 to 15 minutes. Transfer to a wire rack to cool. (The bread will continue to crisp as it cools.)

Meanwhile, for the vinaigrette, in a small bowl whisk together the remaining ½ cup olive oil with the vinegar, garlic, mustard, salt, and black pepper.

In a large bowl, combine the tomatoes, cucumber, basil, onion, and capers; gently toss to combine. Add the bread cubes and gently toss to combine. Drizzle salad with the vinaigrette, and toss to coat. Let stand for 30 minutes for the flavors to blend.

WALDORF SALAD

Among the many locales George wants to visit during his honeymoon, he and Mary are excited to spend a whole week in New York City, to stay at the highest hotels—which might include the Waldorf Astoria, the home of this iconic salad. While their travel plans are not to be, Mary Bailey re-creates their honeymoon at the Waldorf Hotel on Sycamore Lane—their new home—where she gives George a taste of the trip that never was with her own unique take on the iconic salad. Substitute mayonnaise for walnut oil for a version closer to the original recipe.

| YIELD: 6 TO 8 SERVINGS | ACTIVE: 20 MINUTES | TOTAL: 20 MINUTES |

½ cup walnuts

4 large Granny Smith apples, unpeeled

2 tablespoons fresh lemon juice

1 cup chopped celery

2 green onions, chopped

½ cup dried cranberries

⅓ cup walnut oil

3 tablespoons sherry vinegar

In a small skillet, toast the walnuts over medium-low heat, stirring occasionally, until the nuts become fragrant and start to brown, about 5 minutes. Remove to a plate to cool, then chop coarsely.

Halve and core the apples, then cut into ½-inch pieces. In a large bowl, combine the apples with the lemon juice. Add the celery, green onions, cranberries, and toasted walnuts. Add the walnut oil and vinegar, toss to mix, and serve.

ROASTED GARLIC MASHED POTATOES

A must-have for any celebration, this hearty mashed potato dish is a guaranteed hit. It certainly keeps the Bailey family warm and fed during many a snowy night. Serve it with Classic Holiday Roast Turkey (page 67) or Glazed Holiday Ham (page 65).

| YIELD: 6 SERVINGS | ACTIVE: 30 MINUTES | TOTAL: 50 MINUTES |

1 head garlic

1 tablespoon olive oil

3 pounds baking potatoes such as Yukon gold or russet potatoes

½ cup unsalted butter, at room temperature, plus more for serving

½ cup whole milk, warmed

3 tablespoons fresh chives, minced

Salt and freshly ground black pepper

Preheat the oven to 400°F. Slice the head of garlic in half crosswise, drizzle the halves with the olive oil, wrap them in aluminum foil, and place in a small, shallow pan. Bake until the cloves are soft, about 35 minutes. While the garlic is roasting, start making the potatoes.

Peel the potatoes and roughly chop into large pieces. Add the potatoes to a large saucepan, then add water to fully submerge the potatoes. Salt the water, cover the pan, and bring to a boil over high heat. Uncover, reduce the heat to medium-low, and simmer until the potatoes are tender when pierced with a knife, about 20 minutes. Drain well, and place the potatoes in a large heatproof bowl.

Mash the potatoes with a potato masher. Alternatively, you can use a potato ricer or a hand mixer to create fluffier texture. Cut the butter into slices and scatter over the potatoes. Squeeze the softened cloves of garlic from their papery skins into the potatoes, then whisk in the butter and enough of the milk to give the potatoes the texture you like.

Mix in the chives, and season to taste with salt and pepper. Transfer to a warmed serving bowl, and serve at once with additional butter, if desired.

ROASTED KOHLRABI WITH BROWN BUTTER

Kohlrabi—a funny-looking, crisp-textured, and tentacled orb that tastes a bit like broccoli stem (slightly sweet and delicately peppery)—is easy to grow, making it a staple in wartime Victory gardens. Commonly eaten boiled or steamed and tossed in cream sauce, it's even better roasted and drizzled with nutty brown butter.

YIELD: 4 TO 6 SERVINGS	ACTIVE: 15 MINUTES	TOTAL: 40 MINUTES

2 pounds kohlrabi, peeled, quartered, and cut into 1-inch pieces (about 5 cups)

1 tablespoon olive oil

1 teaspoon kosher salt

½ teaspoon freshly ground black pepper

½ cup (1 stick) unsalted butter, sliced

Chopped fresh flat-leaf parsley

Preheat the oven to 400°F. Place the kohlrabi on a large rimmed baking sheet. Lightly coat with the olive oil, then season with salt and black pepper. Roast until tender and starting to brown, turning once, 30 to 35 minutes.

Place a small heavy-bottomed saucepan over medium heat. Add the butter and cook, whisking frequently, until the melted (butter will briefly foam). Continue heating and whisking until the butter turns light golden brown color and has a nutty aroma. Immediately remove pan from the heat, and pour brown the butter into a bowl.

To serve, spoon brown butter over the kohlrabi and sprinkle with parsley. Store any leftover brown butter in an airtight container in the refrigerator for up to 1 week.

CORN MUFFINS

When the Baileys gather for a send-off dinner on the eve of George's much-anticipated trip to Europe, passing around a platter of freshly made corn muffins, nobody could know what the future holds—only that it is bright. And while things don't turn out as planned for George, they ultimately turn out exactly as they were meant to. Moist and tangy from buttermilk, these muffins can be served warm with butter and honey, and they pair well with peas.

YIELD: 12 MUFFINS	ACTIVE: 15 MINUTES	TOTAL: 30 MINUTES

½ cup unsalted butter, melted and cooled slightly, plus more for pan
1 cup yellow cornmeal
1 cup all-purpose flour
⅓ cup granulated sugar
1 tablespoon baking powder
½ teaspoon salt
⅔ cup buttermilk
2 large eggs

Preheat the oven to 375°F. Lightly butter twelve 2½-inch muffin cups.

In a large bowl, stir together the cornmeal, flour, sugar, baking powder, and salt. In a medium bowl, whisk together the buttermilk, melted butter, and eggs. Pour the buttermilk mixture into the cornmeal mixture, and stir just until combined (do not overmix). Divide batter evenly among prepared muffin cups.

Bake until a toothpick inserted in the center of a muffin comes out clean, about 15 minutes. Cool in the pan on a wire rack for 10 minutes.

DEVILED EGGS

A perennial favorite, classic deviled eggs are a welcome component of any appetizer spread, and Mary Bailey would relish serving these delicious bites to her friends and family. Though labeled "devilish," this dish is as tasty as anything Clarence could have brought from heaven.

YIELD: 16 DEVILED EGGS	ACTIVE: 25 MINUTES	TOTAL: 25 MINUTES

8 large eggs

⅓ cup mayonnaise

1 teaspoon minced fresh chives, plus more for garnish

1 teaspoon minced fresh flat-leaf parsley, plus more for garnish

Zest of 1 lemon

Kosher salt and freshly ground black pepper

Paprika

To hard-boil the eggs, place them in a saucepan just large enough to hold them. Add enough cold water to cover by 1 inch, and bring to a boil over high heat. Remove the pan from the heat and cover. Let stand for 15 minutes. Drain the eggs, then immediately transfer to a bowl of ice water, and let cool completely.

Peel the eggs, being careful not to tear the whites. Using a sharp, thin-bladed knife, cut each egg in half lengthwise. Remove the yolks, and set aside the egg white halves. In a small bowl, mash the yolks with a masher or a fork. For an even fluffier filling, rub the yolks through a coarse-mesh sieve into a bowl. Add the mayonnaise, chives, parsley, and lemon zest, and whisk together until light and fluffy. Season to taste with salt, black pepper, and paprika, and whisk again.

Spoon the yolk mixture into a pastry bag fitted with a medium plain tip. Alternatively, place a plastic zip-top bag in a wide-mouthed glass, and fold the edges of the bag down. Fill the bag with the yolk mixture, seal the bag, then snip one corner off the bottom of the bag.

Arrange the egg halves, hollow-sides up, on a platter. Pipe the yolk mixture into the egg white halves. Cover lightly with plastic wrap, and refrigerate until chilled, about 1 hour and up to 8 hours before serving.

Garnish with additional herbs, and serve chilled.

MACARONI AND CHEESE

George Bailey has encountered more than his share of hectic times, and on his most trying day, he worries about how drafty and cold his house is after daughter Zuzu falls ill. This hearty macaroni and cheese recipe is warm and comforting and will make anyone feel better, even on their worst day.

YIELD: 6 SERVINGS	ACTIVE: 20 MINUTES	TOTAL: 45 MINUTES

4 tablespoons butter, plus more for dish

1 pound elbow macaroni

Salt and freshly ground black pepper

¼ cup all-purpose flour

½ teaspoon sweet paprika

½ teaspoon Dijon mustard

2 cups whole milk

1 cup half-and-half

1½ cups shredded Gruyère cheese

1½ cups shredded white cheddar cheese

2 tablespoons minced chives

Preheat the oven to 375°F. Butter a 9-by-13-inch baking dish and set aside.

Bring a large saucepan of salted water to a boil. Add the macaroni and cook, stirring occasionally, until not quite al dente, about 2 minutes less than the package directions. Drain and transfer to a large bowl.

Melt the butter in the saucepan over medium-high heat. Add the flour, paprika, and mustard and cook, stirring well, until no dry flour remains, 1 to 3 minutes. Pour a cup of the milk into the roux, and whisk until combined. Repeat with the remaining milk and half-and-half, then add a generous pinch salt, and bring to a boil. Simmer, whisking frequently to smooth out any lumps, 4 to 5 minutes. Remove from the heat.

Add a pinch of pepper and 1 cup each of the Gruyère and cheddar. Stir until smooth. Pour the cheese sauce onto the macaroni, add the chives, and mix well. Transfer to the prepared dish, and top with the remaining cheeses. Bake until the top is lightly browned and the sauce is bubbly, 25 to 30 minutes. Let stand for 5 minutes before serving.

CHESTNUT DRESSING

Two of the most popular bread-based side dishes appearing on holiday tables in Bedford Falls are oyster dressing and chestnut dressing—dishes baked alongside as a casserole, not to be mistaken for turkey stuffing. Sweet and buttery roasted chestnuts give this dressing richness and flavor. Serve with pork roast, roast chicken, or turkey.

YIELD: 10 SERVINGS	ACTIVE: 25 MINUTES	TOTAL: 1 HOUR 35 MINUTES

Butter, for dish

4 cups cubed day-old white bread (such as country-style white, ciabatta, or focaccia), crusts removed

4 cups cubed day-old corn bread

1 pound bulk mild Italian sausage

1 large yellow onion, chopped

2 stalks celery, chopped

1 teaspoon kosher salt

1/4 teaspoon freshly ground black pepper

1 cup quartered roasted and peeled chestnuts*

1/2 cup lightly packed chopped fresh herbs, such as parsley, sage, rosemary, and thyme

1 teaspoon lemon zest

2 cups low-sodium chicken stock or broth

Preheat the oven to 350°F. Butter a 9-by-13-inch baking dish.

Spread the white bread and corn bread cubes in a single layer on a large rimmed baking sheet. Bake until dry to the touch and golden brown, 20 to 25 minutes.

In a large skillet, cook the sausage over medium heat until cooked through, stirring occasionally, 8 to 10 minutes. Transfer to a large bowl.

In the same skillet, cook the onion and celery in the sausage drippings over medium heat until tender, about 5 minutes. Season with salt and black pepper. Transfer to the bowl with the sausage. Add the bread cubes, chestnuts, herbs, and lemon zest; toss to combine. Pour the stock over the dressing, and gently stir to combine. Transfer to the prepared baking dish.

Bake, covered, for 30 minutes. Uncover, and bake until browned, 20 to 30 minutes.

*Tip: You can purchase good quality vacuum-packed or jarred whole chestnuts. To prepare your own chestnuts, preheat the oven to 450°F. With a sharp knife, cut an X on the round side of each chestnut. Spread chestnuts in a single layer on a large rimmed baking sheet; add 1/4 cup water. Roast until the shells open where cut, about 10 minutes. Remove from the oven, and cover with a towel to keep warm. Peel chestnuts while warm.

CANDIED YAMS

No marshmallows, no nuts, and no fancy toppings—just the flavor of yams sweetened with brown sugar and spiced with ginger, vanilla, cinnamon, nutmeg, and butter, then baked and basted with the glossy syrup that forms. Try them with Glazed Holiday Ham (page 65).

YIELD: 6 SERVINGS	ACTIVE: 15 MINUTES	TOTAL: 45 MINUTES

3 large yams (about 1½ pounds), peeled and cut into 1-inch pieces

½ cup orange juice

½ cup packed dark brown sugar

1 teaspoon grated fresh ginger

½ teaspoon kosher salt

½ teaspoon vanilla extract

½ teaspoon ground cinnamon

¼ teaspoon ground nutmeg

8 tablespoons salted butter (1 stick), coarsely chopped

Preheat the oven to 350°F. In a large saucepan over medium-high heat, place the yams in enough water to cover and cook just until beginning to soften (but not fully cooked), about 10 minutes. Drain the yams; reserve ¼ cup cooking water.

Transfer the yams to an 8-by-8-inch baking dish, spreading evenly. In a medium bowl, stir together the reserved cooking water, orange juice, brown sugar, ginger, salt, vanilla, cinnamon, and nutmeg until the sugar is dissolved. Pour the sugar mixture over the yams, and top with the butter.

Bake until the yams are tender, spooning sauce over the yams once, about 15 minutes. Remove from oven, and spoon sauce over yams. Let stand 5 minutes before serving.

HERBED TURKEY GRAVY

This gravy is the perfect accompaniment to the Classic Holiday Roast Turkey (page 67). The sage and thyme from the turkey are echoed in this recipe for a great complementary combination—just like brothers George and Harry.

YIELD: 4 CUPS	ACTIVE: 15 MINUTES	TOTAL: 15 MINUTES

Reserved pan drippings from Classic Holiday Roast Turkey (page 67)

5 tablespoons all-purpose flour

¼ cup dry white wine

¼ cup water

4 cups chicken or turkey stock

2 teaspoons fresh sage, chopped

2 teaspoons fresh thyme, chopped

Salt and freshly ground black pepper

1 to 2 tablespoons dry sherry (optional)

Skim off the fat from the pan drippings, reserving 4 to 5 tablespoons of the fat. Reserve the pan juices separately. (If you haven't made the turkey yet or don't have any pan drippings, replace the drippings with butter, and replace the pan juices with chicken or turkey stock.)

Place the roasting pan on the stove top over medium-high heat, and add the reserved fat. Sprinkle the flour into the pan, and whisk the fat and flour together until the mixture bubbles, about 1 minute. Add the wine and water to deglaze the pan, stirring to dislodge any browned bits from the pan bottom, then remove from the heat.

Add the reserved juices, 3½ cups of the stock, and the fresh herbs. Continue cooking over medium-low heat, whisking often until smooth and thickened enough to coat the back of a wooden spoon, about 2 minutes. Add the remaining stock as needed to reach the desired consistency. Season with salt and pepper to taste.

For a smoother gravy, pour the gravy through a fine-mesh sieve into a warmed gravy boat. Stir in the sherry, if using, and serve immediately.

APPLE-CRANBERRY SAUCE

This cranberry sauce is made all the more delightful by the addition of apples for a bit more texture. The bright red sauce is the perfect accompaniment to any holiday table, sure to get your guests into the Christmas spirit!

YIELD: 6 TO 8 SERVINGS	ACTIVE: 10 MINUTES	TOTAL: 30 MINUTES + COOLING

1 orange

1 Granny Smith or tart green apple, peeled and finely chopped

3 cups fresh cranberries

1¼ cups sugar

½ teaspoon ground cinnamon

¼ teaspoon ground cloves

Using a vegetable peeler, remove the orange zest from the orange in long strips. Halve the orange, and squeeze the juice into a bowl, discarding any seeds. Place the orange zest strips in a small saucepan with 2 cups water, and bring to a boil over high heat. Boil until the zest has softened, about 10 minutes, then drain.

When the orange zest is cool enough to handle, finely chop it. In a saucepan, combine the zest, juice, apple, cranberries, sugar, cinnamon, and cloves. Place over medium-high heat and bring to a boil. Reduce the heat to medium-low, cover partially, and simmer gently until the mixture is thickened, the apple is tender, and the cranberries have burst, 10 to 15 minutes.

Transfer the sauce to a bowl, and let cool before serving. The sauce can also be covered and refrigerated for up to 1 day; bring back to room temperature before serving.

ENTRÉES

CACIO E PEPE 45

CHICKEN NOODLE SOUP 47

WELSH RAREBIT WITH ROASTED TOMATO 49

TUNA MELT SANDWICH 50

SANDWICH FOR ONE 51

BOARDING HOUSE HASH 53

CABBAGE ROLLS 55

TORTINO 57

PORK ROAST WITH APPLES AND FENNEL 59

PHONOGRAPH FOWL 61

OVEN-BRAISED CORNED BEEF WITH MUSTARD SAUCE 63

GLAZED HOLIDAY HAM 65

CLASSIC HOLIDAY ROAST TURKEY 67

CACIO E PEPE

We don't know from where in Italy the Martini family emigrated, but we do know they arrived without much to their name—at least not at first. This ancient Roman pasta dish exemplifies la cucina povera *("cooking of the poor" or "peasant cooking"). Cucina povera is simply delicious food made from humble ingredients—in this case, spaghetti, butter, cracked black pepper, and cheese. Starch-rich pasta cooking water together with butter and cheese create a silky sauce, while the pepper spikes it with a bit of heat. The name, translated to "cheese and pepper," says it all.*

YIELD: 4 SERVINGS	ACTIVE: 10 MINUTES	TOTAL: 15 MINUTES

Kosher salt

1 pound dried spaghetti

5 tablespoons unsalted butter, sliced

2 teaspoons freshly cracked black pepper, plus more for serving

3 ounces Pecorino Romano, finely grated (1 cup), plus more for serving

Chopped fresh flat-leaf parsley, for garnish

Bring a large pot of salted water to a boil over medium-high heat. Add the pasta and cook, stirring occasionally, until al dente, about 10 minutes. Drain, reserving ½ cup pasta water. (You might not need all of the pasta water.)

Meanwhile, in a large skillet over medium-low heat, melt 3 tablespoons of the butter. Add the black pepper and cook, stirring, until pepper is fragrant and butter is just starting to sizzle, about 1 minute. Add 3 tablespoons of the pasta water to the skillet, and bring to a simmer. Using tongs, transfer the pasta and remaining 2 tablespoons butter to the skillet. Toss pasta to coat. Reduce the heat to low, and sprinkle with the cheese, tossing with tongs until the cheese is melted. Add additional water, 1 tablespoon at a time, until the sauce is creamy. Season to taste with salt.

Serve immediately with additional black pepper and cheese. Sprinkle servings with parsley, if desired.

CHICKEN NOODLE SOUP

When the world has you down, you're under the weather, or you simply live in a big, old, drafty house, nothing comforts, cures, and warms the body and soul like homemade chicken noodle soup. Pair this hearty soup with a simple side salad, tender rolls, or warm Corn Muffins (page 33) for a complete meal.

YIELD: 6 SERVINGS	ACTIVE: 30 MINUTES	TOTAL: 2 HOURS

FOR THE STOCK:

3½ pound whole chicken, giblets discarded

2 carrots, cut into 2-inch pieces

3 stalks celery, cut into 2-inch pieces

1 large yellow onion, cut into 6 wedges

4 to 6 large cloves garlic, smashed

8 sprigs fresh parsley

6 sprigs fresh thyme

4 sprigs fresh dill

2 bay leaves

2 teaspoons kosher salt

1 teaspoon black peppercorns

FOR THE SOUP:

2 tablespoons olive oil

1 medium yellow onion, chopped

2 cloves garlic, minced

3 medium carrots, cut into ½-inch pieces

2 stalks celery, cut into ½-inch pieces

2 quarts reserved homemade stock

4 fresh thyme sprigs

1 bay leaf

12 ounces frozen home-style egg noodles or 2 cups dried wide egg noodles

1½ to 2 cups reserved shredded cooked chicken

Kosher salt and freshly ground black pepper

¼ cup finely chopped fresh flat-leaf parsley

To make the stock, in a large stockpot over medium heat, place the chicken, carrot, celery, onion and cold water just to cover. Add the garlic, parsley, thyme, dill, bay leaves, salt, and peppercorns. Cook until water comes to a boil. Reduce the heat and simmer, partially covered, until a meat thermometer registers 170°F when inserted in the breast, 1 to 1½ hours (add more water if necessary to keep chicken and vegetables just covered).

Carefully transfer the chicken to a cutting board. When cool enough to handle, remove and discard the skin and bones. Shred the meat; reserve 1½ to 2 cups for the soup. Place remaining meat in an airtight container, and refrigerate for up to 3 days or freeze up to 3 months.

Meanwhile, strain the stock through a fine-mesh sieve into another pot. Discard the solids. Reserve 2 quarts stock for the chicken noodle soup, and pour remaining stock into an airtight container, and refrigerate up to 3 days or freeze up to 3 months.

To make the soup, in a large saucepan or stockpot over medium heat, heat the oil and cook the onion, garlic, carrot, and celery until tender, 4 to 5 minutes. Add the stock, thyme, and bay leaf, and bring to a boil. Add the noodles; reduce the heat and simmer until the noodles are tender, about 20 minutes for frozen noodles and 5 minutes for dried noodles. Remove and discard the thyme and bay leaf. Add the reserved chicken, and stir to combine. Cook until heated through, about 5 minutes. Add salt and black pepper to taste. Sprinkle with parsley.

WELSH RAREBIT WITH ROASTED TOMATO

The recipe for this classic British dish of beer-cheese sauce ladled over toasted bread is inspired by one found in the original 1931 edition of The Joy of Cooking, *making it a favorite among Bedford Falls residents. That recipe called for the sauce to be made in a double boiler with just cheese, butter, beer, and an egg. It's more common and probably easier to make it starting with a roux, as is done here. The addition of a roasted tomato on the side helps cut the richness of the sauce.*

YIELD: 4 SERVINGS	ACTIVE: 20 MINUTES	TOTAL: 20 MINUTES

4 small tomatoes

¾ teaspoon kosher salt

¾ teaspoon freshly ground black pepper, plus more for garnishing

2 tablespoons unsalted butter

2 tablespoons all-purpose flour

2 teaspoons dry mustard

2 teaspoons Worcestershire sauce

⅛ teaspoon ground cayenne pepper

1 cup porter or stout beer

8 ounces aged cheddar cheese, shredded

4 slices sourdough or country bread, toasted

Adjust the oven rack to the center position. Preheat the oven to 375°F.

Slice a quarter inch off the top of each tomato. Place tomatoes in an 8-by-8-inch baking dish; sprinkle with ¼ teaspoon of the salt and ¼ teaspoon of the black pepper. Bake until tomatoes are soft, about 30 minutes.

Meanwhile, in a medium saucepan over low heat, melt the butter. Whisk the flour into the butter and cook, whisking constantly, until smooth, about 2 minutes. (Do not let the flour brown.) Whisk in the mustard, Worcestershire sauce, the remaining ½ teaspoon salt, the remaining ½ teaspoon black pepper, and cayenne until smooth. Add the porter, and whisk until well combined. Gradually add the cheese, stirring constantly, until melted and sauce is smooth and thick, 3 to 4 minutes.

Place one toasted bread slice on each of four plates; place one tomato next to the bread. Spoon sauce on top of the bread. Lightly sprinkle with additional freshly ground black pepper.

TUNA MELT SANDWICH

Tuna sandwiches with mayonnaise were a popular way to reuse various food scraps so nothing went to waste. This was especially important when wartime rationing was enacted: Fresh ingredients were hard to come by, and Americans were encouraged to support the war effort by reducing their own consumption. This toasty, rich, and gooey tuna melt is sure to hit the spot, celebrating the canned fish and using up small bits of veggies that might otherwise go wasted.

YIELD: 4 SANDWICHES	ACTIVE: 15 MINUTES	TOTAL: 15 MINUTES

Three 6-ounce cans white albacore tuna packed in oil or water, well drained

½ cup mayonnaise

½ cup minced celery

¼ cup minced yellow or red onion

2 tablespoons minced fresh flat-leaf parsley

Freshly ground black pepper

8 large slices firm white sandwich bread

8 slices tomato

6 ounces cheddar cheese, thinly sliced

Preheat broiler. Place the tuna in a medium bowl. Add the mayonnaise, celery, onion, and parsley and stir well. Season with pepper.

Arrange the bread slices on a rimmed baking sheet and broil, turning once, until lightly browned on both sides, about 1 minute total. Spread the tuna mixture on four of the toasted bread slices. Place the tomato slices and cheese on the sandwiches. Return the sandwiches to the broiler, and broil until the cheese is melted, about 1 minute more. Top with the remaining bread slices. Serve immediately.

SANDWICH FOR ONE

Mary Bailey's life is filled with love, laughter, friends and family, but when Clarence shows George a world in which he doesn't exist, George is horrified to realize he is a complete stranger to Mary, and she never married. In this alternate world, instead of serving a platter of deviled eggs to those dearest to her, she might have found herself making a single sandwich to snack on while she closed up the library.

YIELD: 1 SANDWICH	ACTIVE: 10 MINUTES	TOTAL: 10 MINUTES

½ to 1 cup leftover Deviled Eggs (page 34)

½ small stalk celery, finely chopped

1 green onion, white and green parts, finely chopped

1 teaspoon Dijon mustard

2 slices white bread

1 leaf butter lettuce

Mayonnaise

Place the leftover deviled eggs, celery, green onion, and mustard in a small bowl. Stir to combine, breaking up some of the egg whites.

Spread one of the bread slices with the egg salad; top with a lettuce leaf. Spread the additional mayonnaise on the remaining slice of bread; place, mayonnaise-side down, on the filling.

Tip: If you find yourself fortunate enough to have friends and family over, feel free to double or even quadruple this recipe to make additional sandwiches.

BOARDING HOUSE HASH

George must break through a lot of darkness to see the light. There is perhaps no darker moment than when he visits his childhood home—now Ma Bailey's Boarding House—and his own mother denies his existence. But it is also one moment of many that leads to his declaring, "I want to live again!" The base recipe of this hash can go two ways—a dark version with leftover roast or sausage, or a light version with sunny-side up eggs baked into it.

YIELD: 4 SERVINGS	ACTIVE: 15 MINUTES	TOTAL: 45 MINUTES

3 tablespoons olive oil

3 Yukon gold potatoes (1¼ to 1½ pounds), cut into ¼-inch cubes

1 small yellow onion, chopped

1 red, yellow, or green bell pepper, chopped

3 cloves garlic, minced

1 teaspoon kosher salt

¼ teaspoon coarsely ground black pepper

FOR THE LIGHT VERSION:

4 eggs

Chopped fresh parsley, for garnish

Hot sauce, for serving (optional)

FOR THE DARK VERSION:

1½ cups lightly packed shredded leftover beef or pork roast (or 8 ounces Italian sausage or chorizo, cooked and crumbled)

Chopped fresh parsley, for garnish

Chopped fresh chives, for garnish

In a large oven-safe skillet over medium-high, heat the oil, and cook the potatoes, onion, and bell pepper until tender, 8 to 10 minutes. Add the garlic, salt, and black pepper, and cook until fragrant, 1 to 2 minutes.

To make the light version, adjust an oven rack to the middle position. Preheat the oven to 400°F. Make four indentations in the hash, and carefully crack one egg into each indentation. Transfer the skillet to the oven. Bake until the egg whites are set, 3 to 4 minutes. Sprinkle with additional coarsely ground black pepper and fresh parsley. Serve with hot sauce if desired.

To make the dark version, add the leftover roast or sausage to the skillet with the potato hash. Heat through on the stove, then top with parsley and chives. Serve warm.

CABBAGE ROLLS

The Old Granville House has plenty of elements in need of repair. George constantly contends with the fussy loose knob on his banister that regularly comes off its post. He ultimately comes to appreciate his house and all its imperfections—including the broken staircase.

This cabbage roll recipe may also be a bit fussy, but with its festive color scheme—green cabbage rolls smothered in a savory red sauce—this old-fashioned dish has become a holiday classic over the decades. The sauce and filling can be made a day ahead of when you plan to assemble and bake it.

YIELD: 6 SERVINGS	ACTIVE: 20 MINUTES	TOTAL: 1 HOUR 40 MINUTES

FOR THE TOMATO SAUCE:
2 tablespoons olive oil
1 medium yellow onion, chopped (1 cup)
One 28-ounce can crushed tomatoes
2 tablespoons tomato paste
2 tablespoons red wine vinegar
1 tablespoon packed brown sugar
2 cloves garlic, minced
½ teaspoon salt
¼ teaspoon black pepper
1 large head green cabbage, cored

FOR THE FILLING:
1 pound ground beef
½ pound ground pork
½ small yellow onion, finely chopped (¼ cup)
2 eggs, lightly beaten
¼ cup plain dried bread crumbs
¼ cup uncooked white rice
1 teaspoon minced fresh thyme leaves
¾ teaspoon salt
¼ teaspoon black pepper

Preheat the oven to 350°F.

To make the sauce, in a large skillet over medium, heat the oil and cook the onion until tender, about 5 minutes. Add the tomatoes, tomato paste, vinegar, brown sugar, garlic, salt, and black pepper. Bring to a boil; reduce the heat and simmer, uncovered, 20 minutes.

Meanwhile, remove 15 leaves from the cabbage. Bring a large pot of water to a boil; add cabbage leaves a few at a time, and cook until flexible, about 1 minute. Use tongs to remove leaves. When cool enough to handle, use a small knife to trim the tough rib from cabbage leaves. Set aside.

To make the filling, in a large bowl, combine the beef, pork, onion, eggs, bread crumbs, rice, thyme, salt, and black pepper. Add 1 cup sauce, and mix well.

Place 1 cup sauce in the bottom of an 8-by-8-inch baking dish. Spoon ¼ cup of the filling onto smaller leaves and ½ cup of the filling onto the larger leaves at the rib end, and roll, tucking in the sides as you roll.

Arrange rolls in rows, seam-side down, on the sauce in the baking dish. Spoon the remaining sauce over the rolls. Cover the dish with foil.

Bake until the meat is cooked and rice is tender, 1 to 1¼ hours.

TORTINO

Goat cheese and garden vegetables are the star ingredients in this summery frittata-like dish—a favorite of the Martini family, given how versatile it is. Swap out the cheese if you like, or the vegetables, depending on what's in season. It's perfect for brunch with fresh fruit or as a light supper with a crisp green salad.

YIELD: 8 SERVINGS	ACTIVE: 20 MINUTES	TOTAL: 55 MINUTES

3 tablespoons olive oil

1 cup chopped leek, white part only

1 small zucchini, halved lengthwise and chopped (about 6 ounces)

½ cup chopped red bell pepper

2 cloves garlic, minced

1 tablespoon fresh thyme leaves

6 large eggs

4 ounces goat cheese, crumbled

½ cup heavy cream

1 teaspoon kosher salt

½ teaspoon freshly ground black pepper

¼ teaspoon Aleppo pepper or 2 drops hot sauce

½ cup grated Asiago cheese

Preheat the oven to 350°F.

In a 9-inch oven-safe skillet over medium heat, heat the oil and cook the leek, zucchini, bell pepper, and garlic until tender, 4 to 5 minutes. Remove from the heat and add the thyme; stir to combine. Let cool for 10 minutes.

In a medium bowl, whisk together the eggs, goat cheese, heavy cream, salt, black pepper, and Aleppo pepper. Pour over the vegetables in the skillet, and sprinkle with Asiago cheese.

Bake until the eggs are set, about 20 minutes. Cut into wedges and serve warm or at room temperature.

PORK ROAST WITH APPLES AND FENNEL

This spiraled roast, a classic roulade, is filled with a sweet-savory stuffing of apples, fennel, shallot, and thyme—a festive combination that's perfect for any occasion, from Christmas dinner to celebrating Harry's safe return from the war. Serve it with mashed potatoes, sweet or white, and green beans or Brussels sprouts.

YIELD: 8 TO 10 SERVINGS	ACTIVE: 25 MINUTES	TOTAL: 2 HOURS 15 MINUTES

1 tablespoon olive oil

1 tablespoon unsalted butter

2 cups chopped, peeled Granny Smith apples

1 fennel bulb, trimmed, cored, and chopped

1 shallot, finely chopped

1 teaspoon salt

1 teaspoon freshly ground black pepper

¼ cup chopped pecans, toasted

1 tablespoon chopped fresh thyme

One 3-pound boneless pork top loin roast (single loin)

For the stuffing, in a large skillet, heat the oil and butter over medium. Add the apples, fennel, shallot, ½ teaspoon of the salt, and ¼ teaspoon of the black pepper. Cook, stirring occasionally, just until tender, 4 to 5 minutes. Stir in the pecans and thyme.

Preheat the oven to 325°F. Butterfly the pork roast by making a lengthwise cut down the center of the roast, cutting to within half an inch of the other side. Spread the roast open. Place the knife in the V cut, facing it horizontally toward one side of the V, and cut to within half an inch of the side. Repeat on the other side of the V. Spread the roast open, and cover with plastic wrap. Working from the center to the edges, pound the roast with a meat mallet until it is about ¾ inch thick. Remove and discard the plastic wrap.

Season the meat with remaining ½ teaspoon salt and an additional ¼ teaspoon of the black pepper. Spread the stuffing over the roast. Starting from a short side, roll the roast into a spiral. Tie with 100 percent cotton kitchen string in several places to hold the roast together. Sprinkle roast with the remaining ½ teaspoon black pepper.

Place roast on a rack in a shallow roasting pan. Insert an oven-going thermometer into the center of the roast (not in the stuffing). Roast, uncovered, for 1 hour 15 minutes to 1 hour 30 minutes or until thermometer registers 145°F. Remove the roast and cover loosely with foil; let stand for 15 minutes before slicing.

PHONOGRAPH FOWL

It's a testament to the resilience and creativity of a just-married Mary Bailey to turn a record player into a rotisserie to roast a bird for her nuptial feast in the fireplace of her newly acquired fixer-upper. You don't need to do that—or even have a rotisserie—to make this lemon-herb chicken. High heat at the beginning of roasting creates a crisp skin. Lowering the heat to finish cooking keeps the meat luxuriously juicy.

YIELD: 4 TO 6 SERVINGS	ACTIVE: 20 MINUTES	TOTAL: 1 HOUR 35 MINUTES

One 4- to 5-pound whole chicken

2 lemons

3 tablespoons minced fresh flat-leaf parsley

2 tablespoon minced fresh rosemary

1 tablespoon chopped fresh thyme

2 tablespoons olive oil

3 cloves garlic, minced

1 teaspoon kosher salt, plus more to taste

½ teaspoon freshly ground black pepper, plus more to taste

Position a rack in the center of the oven. Preheat the oven to 450°F. Pat the chicken dry with paper towels.

Remove the zest from one of the lemons with a zester. To make the gremolata, in a small bowl, combine the parsley, rosemary, thyme, 1 tablespoon oil, garlic, lemon zest, salt, and black pepper. Loosen the skin on the chicken breast and legs, and spread the gremolata under the skin. Cut the remaining lemon into four wedges and place in the cavity. Skewer the neck of the chicken to the back; tie legs to the tail. Twist the wing tips under the back. Place the chicken, breast-side up, on a rack in a shallow roasting pan. Spread the chicken with the remaining 1 tablespoon oil and season to taste with salt and pepper.

Roast chicken for 20 minutes. Reduce the oven temperature to 375°F. Roast the chicken until a meat thermometer inserted into thickest part of the inner thigh registers 170°F and drumsticks move easily in their sockets, 1¼ to 1½ hours. (Cover with foil to prevent overbrowning after 1 hour if necessary.) Remove from the oven. Cover and let stand 10 minutes before carving.

OVEN-BRAISED CORNED BEEF WITH MUSTARD SAUCE

The Bailey family's Dutch oven is perfect for homey fare. Mary is always pulling delightful warm and fragrant dishes from the oven—something like this braised spiced beef that's slow-cooked until it's butter-knife tender, then served with a mustardy sour cream sauce.

YIELD: 6 SERVINGS	ACTIVE: 20 MINUTES	TOTAL: 4 HOURS

2 bay leaves, crushed

1 tablespoon mustard seeds

1 tablespoon coriander seeds

2 teaspoons black peppercorns

1 teaspoon whole allspice

½ teaspoon fennel seeds

½ teaspoon crushed red pepper

One 3- to 4-pound corned beef brisket

1½ pounds Yukon gold potatoes, quartered

4 carrots or parsnips, peeled, halved lengthwise, and cut into 2-inch pieces

1 large onion, cut into wedges

1 cup sour cream

2 tablespoons prepared horseradish

2 tablespoons Dijon mustard

¼ teaspoon kosher salt

¼ teaspoon freshly ground black pepper

Chopped fresh chives, for garnish

Preheat oven to 325°F.

For the spice mix, in a small bowl, combine the bay leaves, mustard, coriander, peppercorns, allspice, fennel, and crushed red pepper. Lightly crush the spice mix with a mortar and pestle, or add to a spice grinder and pulse once or twice to release the aromatics.

Rinse the brisket under cold water; pat dry with paper towels. (If the brisket comes with a spice packet, discard or save for another use.) Place the brisket, fat-side up, on a rack in a 6-quart Dutch oven. Add approximately 3 cups water to the Dutch oven (do not cover the brisket with water). Pat the spice mix on top of the brisket.

Bake, covered, for 2½ hours. Remove the lid, and add the potatoes, carrots, and onion to the cooking liquid in the pan. Bake until the meat and vegetables are tender, about 1 hour more.

Use a slotted spoon to transfer the vegetables to a serving platter or bowl. Transfer the meat to a cutting board, and let it rest 10 minutes. In a small bowl, stir together the sour cream, horseradish, mustard, salt, and black pepper, then garnish the sauce with the chives. Thinly slice the meat against the grain. Serve the vegetables alongside the meat with the mustard sauce.

GLAZED HOLIDAY HAM

What's more quintessentially holiday than a glorious glazed ham? Start the celebratory spread with Pastry Snails (page 11), then serve with Waldorf Salad (page 28), Candied Yams (page 39), Corn Muffins (page 33), and some steamed and buttered green beans sprinkled with toasted almond slices.

YIELD: 10 TO 12 SERVINGS	ACTIVE: 15 MINUTES	TOTAL: 2 HOURS

One 7- to 9-pound bone-in fully cooked ham

2 tablespoons whole cloves

¼ cup grainy brown mustard

¼ cup orange juice

2 tablespoons mild molasses

2 tablespoons Worcestershire sauce

2 tablespoons packed brown sugar

Preheat the oven to 300°F.

Meanwhile, score the ham by making shallow diagonal cuts in a diamond pattern at 1-inch intervals. Stud the center of each diamond with a clove. Place the ham on a rack in a roasting pan. Insert an oven-safe thermometer into the center of the ham, avoiding the bone. Cover with foil.

Bake for 1 hour 15 minutes. Uncover and bake 20 to 60 minutes more or until the thermometer registers 120°F, brushing the ham with glaze every 10 minutes.

For the glaze, in a small saucepan, stir together the mustard, orange juice, molasses, Worcestershire sauce, and brown sugar. Cook over medium heat, stirring frequently, until the mixture comes to a boil. Reduce the heat, and simmer until thickened, stirring frequently to a glazing consistency, about 10 minutes.

Transfer the ham to a serving platter, and let stand 15 minutes before carving.

CLASSIC HOLIDAY ROAST TURKEY

With an orange-herb butter rubbed under the skin before roasting, and the same butter (with honey added) brushed on the skin during roasting, this turkey takes on a specialness that makes it perfect for a holiday gathering. Reserve the pan drippings to make Herbed Turkey Gravy (page 40), then serve it with Chestnut Dressing (page 37), Apple-Cranberry Sauce (page 41), Roasted Garlic Mashed Potatoes (page 29), and roasted Brussels sprouts. With family and friends to feast with, you'll feel like the richest person in town!

YIELD: 8 TO 10 SERVINGS	ACTIVE: 15 MINUTES	TOTAL: 3 HOURS

One 10- to 12-pound turkey

Kosher salt

Freshly ground black pepper

1 medium orange

½ cup unsalted butter, softened

2 tablespoons finely chopped fresh sage, plus 1 sprig for cavity

1 tablespoon finely chopped fresh thyme, plus 2 sprigs for cavity

1 teaspoon paprika

¼ cup honey

1 apple, quartered

2 stalks celery

1 medium onion, quartered

1 bulb garlic, trimmed to expose cloves

Vegetable oil or unsalted butter, melted

Adjust an oven rack to the lowest position. Preheat the oven to 350°F. Remove the neck and giblets from turkey; reserve for gravy or discard. Pat the turkey skin dry with paper towels. Season the turkey cavity with salt and black pepper.

Remove 2 teaspoons zest from the orange. In a small saucepan, stir together the zest, softened butter, chopped sage, chopped thyme, paprika, ½ teaspoon salt, and ¼ teaspoon black pepper. Loosen the skin on the turkey breast, and spread half the butter mixture under the skin. Stir the honey into remaining butter mixture; set aside.

Cut the orange into wedges and place them in the turkey cavity. Add the apple, celery, onion, garlic, sage sprig, and thyme sprigs to the cavity. Skewer the neck skin to the back. Tuck the drumstick ends under the band of skin across the tail if present. Twist the wing tips under the back. Place the turkey, breast-side up, on a rack in a shallow roasting pan. Brush with oil or melted butter; sprinkle with additional salt and pepper.

Cover the turkey loosely with foil, and roast for 1 hour. Remove the foil and roast until a meat thermometer inserted in the inner thigh and thickest part of the breast registers 170°F, about 1½ hours. (The juices should run clear, and the drumsticks should move easily in their sockets.) During the last 15 minutes of roasting, brush turkey with butter-honey mixture every 5 minutes. Remove the turkey from the oven. Cover it with foil, and let stand 15 to 20 minutes before carving.

DESSERTS

UNCLE BILLY'S PEANUT BRITTLE

Plain peanuts make a wonderful snack any time of year—just ask Uncle Billy—but during the holiday season, they're easily turned into this special crunchy candy treat.

YIELD: 10 SERVINGS   ACTIVE: 20 MINUTES   TOTAL: 40 MINUTES

¼ cup unsalted butter, plus more for pan (no substitutes)

1 cup granulated sugar

½ cup light corn syrup

¼ cup water

⅛ teaspoon salt

1 cup raw peanuts

1 teaspoon vanilla extract

1 teaspoon baking soda

Generously butter a large rimmed baking sheet. In a heavy medium saucepan over medium heat, combine the ¼ cup butter, sugar, corn syrup, water, and salt. Cook, stirring frequently, until a candy thermometer registers 280°F (soft crack stage). Add the peanuts and vanilla and stir constantly, until the thermometer registers 300°F (hard-crack stage).

Immediately stir in the baking soda (mixture will foam). Quickly pour the brittle onto the prepared baking sheet and spread into a thin, even layer. Let stand until cooled completely. Break into large pieces.

ZUZU'S GINGERSNAPS

"Zuzu, Zuzu, my little gingersnap! How do you feel?" George asked this question of his youngest daughter, exuberant at the realization that he'd changed his little corner of the world for the good. Maybe life itself is like a gingersnap—sweet, a little bit spicy, and always a wonderful thing.

YIELD: 60 COOKIES	ACTIVE: 15 MINUTES	TOTAL: 45 MINUTES

Nonstick cooking spray

2¼ cups all-purpose flour

1 tablespoon ground ginger

2 teaspoons baking soda

½ teaspoon freshly ground black pepper

1 teaspoon ground cinnamon

½ teaspoon ground cloves

½ teaspoon salt

¾ cup shortening

1 cup granulated sugar, plus more for rolling

½ teaspoon vanilla extract

⅓ cup molasses

1 large egg

Preheat the oven to 375°F. Lightly coat two baking sheets with cooking spray.

In a small bowl, combine the flour, ginger, baking soda, black pepper, cinnamon, cloves, and salt. Set aside. In a large bowl, beat the shortening, sugar, and vanilla with an electric mixer on medium speed until light and fluffy, about 2 minutes. Add the molasses and egg; beat until well combined. Add the flour mixture to the shortening mixture, and beat until well combined (dough will be stiff).

Add some sugar to a shallow bowl. Shape the dough into 1-inch balls and roll each in sugar. Place dough balls 2 inches apart on prepared baking sheets. Bake until lightly browned, 11 to 13 minutes. Let cool 1 minute, then transfer the cookies to wire racks to cool completely.

VANILLA MOONBEAM PIES

Every bite of these ethereal, marshmallow-creme-filled graham cracker sandwich cookies coated in white chocolate will send you to the moon. No lasso needed.

YIELD: 9 SERVINGS	ACTIVE: 30 MINUTES	TOTAL: 1 HOUR + STANDING

1¼ cups graham cracker crumbs

1 cup all-purpose flour

½ teaspoon baking powder

1 teaspoon baking soda

½ cup packed light brown sugar

6 tablespoons unsalted butter, softened

1 teaspoon vanilla extract

1 large egg

1 egg yolk

1 cup marshmallow creme

Nonstick cooking spray

1 pound white chocolate or vanilla candy melts

Iridescent sanding sugar

Preheat the oven to 350°F. Line two large rimmed baking sheets with parchment paper.

In a small bowl, stir together the graham cracker crumbs, flour, baking powder, and baking soda. In a large bowl, combine the brown sugar and butter; beat with an electric mixer on medium speed until light and fluffy, 2 to 3 minutes. Beat in the vanilla, egg, and egg yolk. Gradually add the graham cracker mixture, and beat just until combined, 1 to 2 minutes (dough may appear crumbly). Using your hands, work the dough into a ball; divide it in half.

Working with one dough ball at a time, roll the dough between sheets of parchment paper to a ¼-inch thickness. Remove the top layer of parchment and use a 2½-inch round cutter to cut the dough into circles. Place 1 inch apart on the prepared baking sheets. Repeat with remaining dough ball for a total of 18 dough circles, rerolling scraps as necessary.

Bake until firm around the edges and the bottoms are golden, 9 to 11 minutes. Transfer to wire racks to cool completely.

Spoon a scant 2 tablespoons marshmallow creme in the center of the flat-side of 9 cookies (do not spread) and top with remaining 9 cookies, flat sides down. Place the cookie sandwiches on a baking sheet, and freeze until the marshmallow creme is firm, 20 to 30 minutes.

Meanwhile, line a large rimmed baking sheet with parchment paper. Coat a wire rack with cooking spray, and place it on the baking sheet. Line a second baking sheet with parchment paper and lightly coat with cooking spray.

Place the white chocolate in a medium microwave-safe bowl. Microwave on medium until melted and smooth, about 2 minutes, stirring every 30 seconds.

One cookie sandwich at a time, roll the side in the melted coating, then spoon the coating over the top and bottom, letting the excess drip off. Transfer to the prepared cooling rack; sprinkle with sanding sugar. Transfer to the oiled parchment paper and let each cookie rest until the coating is set, at least 1 hour.

ANNIE'S MIXED-BERRY PIE

It's June of 1928, and Harry Bailey is graduating high school. Annie—the family's maid and baker extraordinaire—fills the car with her homemade pies to take to the graduation party. This summertime mixed-berry pie is perfect for any celebration, but especially for recognizing your favorite graduate!

YIELD: 1 PIE (8 SERVINGS)	ACTIVE: 30 MINUTES	TOTAL: 1 HOUR 45 MINUTES

FOR THE CRUST:
2½ cups all-purpose flour, plus more for dusting

1 teaspoon kosher salt

½ cup (1 stick) very cold unsalted butter, cut into small pieces

⅓ cup very cold shortening

4 to 6 tablespoons ice water

FOR THE FILLING:
¾ cup granulated sugar

3 tablespoons cornstarch

1 teaspoon lemon zest

¼ to ½ teaspoon ground cinnamon

6 cups fresh blueberries, red raspberries, and/or blackberries*

1 tablespoon unsalted butter, cut into small pieces

1 egg yolk

1 tablespoon heavy cream

1 tablespoon coarse sugar

To make the crust, combine the flour and salt in a food processor and pulse 4 or 5 times to combine. Add the cold butter, and process until the butter mixture resembles coarse crumbs, about 20 seconds. Add the shortening, and pulse until the crumbs are pea size. Add 4 tablespoons ice water and pulse just until the dough is moistened and begins to form a ball. (If the dough appears dry and is not holding together, add more water, 1 tablespoon at a time, and pulse.) Remove the dough from food processor and divide in half, forming two discs. Wrap the discs in plastic, and chill for 30 minutes.

Arrange an oven rack in the center of the oven. Place a foil-lined baking sheet on the rack under the center rack. Preheat the oven to 450°F. On a lightly floured surface, roll one pastry disc into a 12-inch circle. Fold the dough in half and place in the pie plate. Unfold and ease the pastry into the pie plate without stretching it. Trim the pastry even with plate's edge. Refrigerate while making the filling.

For the filling, in a large bowl, stir together the sugar, cornstarch, lemon zest, and cinnamon. Add the berries; toss to coat. Transfer to the pastry-lined pie plate; top with butter. Refrigerate while rolling out the top crust.

For a lattice-top pie,** roll the remaining pastry disc into a 12-inch circle. Cut the pastry into ½-inch-wide strips. Lay half of the pastry strips on top of the filling about 1 inch apart. Fold alternating pastry strips back halfway. Place a strip in the center of the pie across the strips already in place.

Unfold the folded strips. Place another strip across the first set of strips parallel to the strip in the center. Repeat until lattice covers filling. Trim any excess dough from the strips. Press the strip ends into the bottom pastry rim. Fold the bottom pastry over the strip ends; seal and crimp the edge.

In a small bowl, whisk together the egg yolk and cream. Brush the egg wash over pastry, then sprinkle with coarse sugar.

Bake pie for 15 minutes. Reduce oven temperature to 375°F. Bake for 1 hour or until filling is bubbly. If needed to prevent overbrowning, cover the pie loosely with foil for the last 5 to 10 minutes. Cool on a wire rack 2 to 3 hours.

*Note: If fresh berries are unavailable, use frozen berries (do not thaw), and increase the baking time by 10 to 15 minutes or until the filling is bubbly.

**Note: For a double-crust pie, roll the remaining pastry disc into a 12-inch circle. Using a sharp knife, cut slits into the pastry. Place on the filling and trim to ½ inch beyond edge of pie plate. Fold the pastry under the bottom pastry. Seal and crimp the edge. Continue as directed.

COCONUT FUDGE ICEBOX CAKE

In the 1920s and 1930s, modern electric refrigerators began making inroads into American homes, inspiring snack companies to print icebox cake recipes on the backs of chocolate wafer boxes and the like. Then, as now, the base of the classic icebox cake is layers of whipped cream and wafer cookies. Though young Mary Hatch may have not wanted coconuts on her chocolate ice cream, with a nudge from George she discovers how delicious ice cream and coconut are together. Say yes to fudge, and yes to coconuts.

YIELD: 12 SERVINGS	ACTIVE: 30 MINUTES	TOTAL: 8 HOURS 30 MINUTES

2 cups cold heavy cream

¼ cup sugar

1 teaspoon vanilla extract

One 9-ounce package chocolate wafer cookies or one 13-ounce package thin chocolate sandwich cookies

One 12-ounce jar hot fudge sauce

1 cup sweetened shredded coconut, toasted

Shaved coconut, toasted, for garnish

Chill a large bowl and beaters in the freezer for 10 minutes before using. In the chilled bowl, combine the cream, sugar, and vanilla. Beat with an electric mixer on medium speed until stiff peaks form (tips stand straight).

Line a 9-by-5-inch loaf pan with plastic wrap, extending the wrap over edges. Spread ¼ cup of the whipped cream into the prepared loaf pan. Top with a single layer of cookies, 3 tablespoons of the fudge sauce, and ¼ cup of the toasted coconut. Spread ¾ cup whipped cream on the coconut. Top with a single layer of cookies, 3 tablespoons of the fudge sauce, and ¼ cup of the toasted coconut. Repeat layers twice to reach the top edge of the pan, ending with whipped cream. Cover with plastic wrap, and chill in the refrigerator for 8 to 12 hours to allow the cookies to soften. Cover and chill remaining whipped cream.

Remove the plastic wrap from the cake. Invert the cake onto a serving plate; remove pan and plastic wrap. Frost the top with the ¾ cup of the remaining whipped cream. Sprinkle with shaved coconut. Use a serrated knife to slice.

CLARENCE'S ANGEL FOOD CAKE

While it took almost 200 years for Clarence Odbody to earn his wings, we're so glad he finally did, by saving George's life. This heavenly angel food cake celebrates the Bailey family's favorite guardian angel. The tender, ethereal confection is enrobed in fluffy vanilla frosting, dusted with shimmering sugar, and decorated with candy pearls for a celestial effect. Did you hear a bell ring?

YIELD: 10 TO 12 SERVINGS	ACTIVE: 40 MINUTES	TOTAL: 1 HOUR 15 MINUTES

FOR THE CAKE:

1¾ cups granulated sugar

1 cup cake flour, sifted

¼ teaspoon salt

12 egg whites, room temperature

1½ teaspoons cream of tartar

1 teaspoon vanilla extract

FOR THE 7-MINUTE FROSTING:

1½ cups granulated sugar

⅓ cup cold water

2 egg whites

¼ teaspoon cream of tartar or light corn syrup

1 teaspoon vanilla extract

1 to 2 drops blue soft gel paste food coloring, for frosting

White sparkling sugar, for decorating

Blue or white sugar pearls, for decorating

Adjust the oven rack to the middle position. Preheat the oven to 350°F.

To make the cake, in a food processor or blender, pulse the sugar until superfine, 1½ to 2 minutes. Remove 1 cup and set aside. Add the cake flour and salt to the food processor. Pulse just until light and combined, five to six times.

In a large bowl, using a hand mixer or a stand mixer fitted with a whisk attachment, beat the egg whites and cream of tartar on medium-low speed until foamy, about 1 minute. Increase the speed to medium-high and gradually add the 1 cup reserved sugar. Beat until soft peaks form (tips curl), 5 to 6 minutes. Add the vanilla extract and beat just until combined.

In three additions, gradually add the flour mixture to the egg white mixture by hand, gently folding after each addition. Carefully spoon into an ungreased 10-inch tube pan.

Bake until a wooden skewer inserted in the middle comes out clean, rotating the pan once halfway through baking, 40 to 45 minutes. Cool the cake upside-down in the pan on a wire rack for 3 hours. Run a thin knife around the edges and gently tap the pan on the counter until the cake releases; place on a serving plate.

To make the frosting, in the top of a double boiler, combine the sugar, cold water, egg whites, and cream of tartar. Beat with an electric mixer on low speed for 30 seconds. Place over boiling water (the upper pan should not touch the water). Cook, beating constantly with the electric mixer on high speed, until the frosting forms stiff peaks (tips stand straight), about 7 minutes. Remove from the heat; add the vanilla. Beat 2 to 3 minutes more or until frosting reaches spreading consistency.

Divide the frosting between two medium bowls. For very light blue frosting, add the food coloring to the frosting in one of the bowls; gently stir to combine. Starting on the top of the cake, frost the cake in alternating white and blue frosting, using the back of a spoon to create swirls like fluffy clouds. Sprinkle the top with sparkling sugar and sugar pearls.

Slice the cake with a sharp serrated knife. Store the frosted cake in the refrigerator, and serve the same day it is made.

GINGERBREAD LOAF

The holidays just aren't the same without gingerbread, whether in the form of cookies or a wholesome loaf, as is the case here. This recipe is sure to make your holiday celebrations that much more special, just like George Bailey's little gingersnap, Zuzu.

YIELD: 10 TO 12 SERVINGS	ACTIVE: 20 MINUTES	TOTAL: 1 HOUR 35 MINUTES

1 cup (2 sticks) unsalted butter, plus more for pans

3 cups all-purpose flour, plus more for pans

½ teaspoon kosher salt

1 teaspoon baking soda

1 teaspoon ground cinnamon

1 teaspoon ground allspice

2 tablespoon ground ginger

¼ cup peeled and grated fresh ginger

1 cup firmly packed light brown sugar

1 large egg

1 cup light molasses

1 cup buttermilk

Whipped cream, optional

Preheat the oven to 350°F. Butter a 10-inch bundt pan or two 9-by-5-inch loaf pans. Dust lightly with flour and shake out any excess.

In a large bowl, whisk together the flour, salt, baking soda, cinnamon, allspice, ground ginger, and fresh ginger. In another large bowl, using an electric mixer, beat the butter and brown sugar until light and creamy. Beat in the egg. Add the molasses, and beat until well blended, about 2 minutes. Beat in the dry ingredients in three additions alternating with the buttermilk in two additions, beginning and ending with the flour mixture. Pour the batter into the prepared pans.

Bake until a toothpick inserted into the center of the cake comes out clean, about 50 minutes. Let cool in the pan on a wire rack for 10 minutes, then turn out of the pan, slipping a knife between the cake and the pan to loosen any stuck edges. If the cake does not release immediately, let cool for a bit longer. Turn the cake right-side up, and let cool for at least 15 minutes before serving. Serve slices with whipped cream, if you like.

CHOCOLATE CHIP COOKIES

There's nothing that tastes more like home than chocolate chip cookies. Though brothers George and Harry lead very different lives, the two of them share memories of their childhood together, such as these chocolate chip cookies.

YIELD: 48 COOKIES	ACTIVE: 30 MINUTES	TOTAL: 1 HOUR

2¼ cups all-purpose flour

1 teaspoon baking soda

1 teaspoon salt

1 cup (2 sticks) unsalted butter

⅔ cup firmly packed light brown sugar

⅔ cup granulated sugar

1 large whole egg plus 2 large egg yolks

2 teaspoons vanilla extract

12 ounces (about 1 cup) semisweet chocolate, roughly chopped

Preheat the oven to 350°F. Line two cookie sheets with parchment paper. In a medium bowl, whisk together the flour, baking soda, and salt. In a large bowl, using an electric mixer, beat the butter, brown sugar, and granulated sugar on medium speed until light and fluffy, about 3 minutes.

Add the egg, egg yolks, and vanilla, and beat on low speed until combined. Turn off the mixer, and scrape down the bowl with a rubber spatula. Add the flour mixture, and beat on low speed just until blended.

Turn off the mixer, add the chocolate chunks, and stir with a wooden spoon until the chocolate is evenly mixed into the dough.

Drop rounded tablespoons of the dough onto the prepared cookie sheets, spaced about 1 inch apart. Bake each cookie sheet one at a time until the cookies are golden brown, 8 to 10 minutes. Remove each sheet from the oven, and set it on a wire rack. Let cool for 5 minutes, then use a metal spatula to move the cookies directly to the rack. Repeat to bake the rest of the cookies. Let cool until just barely warm and serve.

MELTAWAY MOON COOKIES

You don't need to lasso and swallow the moon to have these buttery, pecan-studded, powdered-sugar-coated cookies dissolve in your mouth. A plate of these may make moonbeams of delight shoot out of your fingers, toes, and even the ends of your hair—and they are certainly sure to win over your sweetheart.

YIELD: 48 COOKIES	ACTIVE: 20 MINUTES	TOTAL: 50 MINUTES

1 cup unsalted butter, softened

½ cup powdered sugar, plus more for coating

1 teaspoon vanilla extract

¼ teaspoon kosher salt

2 cups all-purpose flour

1½ cups finely chopped pecans, toasted

In a large bowl, beat butter and powdered sugar with an electric mixer on medium speed until well combined. Add the vanilla and salt and beat until combined. Add the flour and pecans and beat just until combined. Shape dough into a ball and wrap in plastic. Chill until firm enough to shape, 30 minutes.

Preheat the oven to 350°F. Shape the dough into 1-inch balls. Place 1 inch apart on ungreased baking sheets. Bake until lightly browned, 11 to 12 minutes. Transfer to wire racks to cool until easy to handle but still warm. Place powdered sugar in a shallow dish and roll the cookies in it to coat. Return cookies to the wire rack to cool completely.

Add more powdered sugar to a large resealable plastic bag. Add cookies to the bag a few at a time and gently shake to coat.

POTTER'S PRUNE CLAFOUTI

If ever there was a living, breathing, human embodiment of a prune, it would have to be the vile and ill-tempered Henry F. Potter. This classic French dessert of fruit (in this case, brandied prunes) baked in a thick, flan-like batter sweetens things up considerably.

YIELD: 8 SERVINGS	ACTIVE: 15 MINUTES	TOTAL: 1 HOUR 15 MINUTES

2 cups pitted prunes

1 cup brandy

2 tablespoons unsalted butter, melted, plus more for the dish

3 large eggs

6 tablespoons sugar

1 teaspoon vanilla extract

½ cup all-purpose flour

1 cup whole milk

Pinch of salt

Powdered sugar, for dusting

Preheat the oven to 350°F. In a small bowl, combine the prunes and brandy. Let soak for 30 minutes. Drain the prunes.

Butter a 9-inch round ceramic gratin baking dish or cast-iron skillet. In a medium bowl, whisk together the eggs, sugar, remaining 2 tablespoons butter, and vanilla. Gradually add the flour and whisk until smooth. Whisk in the milk and salt until light and smooth, 2 to 3 minutes. Pour the batter into the gratin. Scatter the prunes on the batter.

Bake until clafouti is set and golden brown, about 30 minutes. Let cool slightly. Dust with powdered sugar. Cut into wedges.

COCONUT RICE PUDDING

George loved coconut—a product of Tahiti—partly because it symbolized adventures beyond Bedford Falls. He even insisted on topping off young Mary Hatch's ice cream with it when he was a youngster working at Mr. Gower's drugstore and soda fountain. Little did George know that his greatest adventure would in fact be his life with Mary. George may never have traveled to Tahiti, but this creamy pudding with mango and coconut is the next best thing!

YIELD: 4 SERVINGS	ACTIVE: 40 MINUTES	TOTAL: 40 MINUTES

2 cups cold unsalted cooked medium white rice

2 cups whole milk

One 14-ounce can unsweetened coconut milk

⅓ cup granulated sugar

¼ teaspoon salt

¼ teaspoon ground cardamom

½ teaspoon vanilla extract

2 ripe mangos, seeded, skin removed, and diced

½ cup shaved coconut, toasted

In a heavy 3-quart saucepan over medium-low heat, simmer the rice, milk, coconut milk, sugar, salt, and cardamom, uncovered, until thickened and creamy, stirring frequently, about 30 minutes. Stir in the vanilla. Top portions with mango and coconut and serve warm.

GEORGE AND MARY'S WEDDING CAKE

Although it wasn't the honeymoon they'd hoped for, moving into the old Granville house on their wedding night means coming full circle for George and Mary. According to local legend, if you threw a rock at the abandoned home and broke a window, you'd be granted one wish. Walking with George after the high school graduation party, Mary had wished for that very thing—to live in that "drafty old house" with him. Maybe Mary didn't foresee the bank run, or any of the hardships she'd face, but she did see a wonderful life with George, and it starts with their "Bridal Suite"—a makeshift feast, and a petite wedding cake. That cake was a precursor to red velvet— what was then called a "mahogany cake," because of its faint red hue due to a chemical reaction between vinegar and cocoa powder. This version, in the modern style, calls for red food coloring.

YIELD: 4 TO 6 SERVINGS	ACTIVE: 20 MINUTES	TOTAL: 50 MINUTES + COOLING

FOR THE CAKE:
¼ cup canola oil, plus more for greasing
½ cup plus 1 tablespoon cake flour or ½ cup all-purpose flour
½ cup granulated sugar
1 tablespoon unsweetened cocoa powder
¼ teaspoon salt
1 large egg, at room temperature
2 teaspoons red food coloring
1 teaspoon vanilla
¼ cup buttermilk
½ teaspoon white vinegar
¼ teaspoon baking soda

FOR THE FROSTING:
6 tablespoons shortening
6 ounces cream cheese
1½ teaspoons clear vanilla
4½ cups powdered sugar

To make the cake, preheat the oven to 350°F. Lightly grease one 6-by-2-inch round cake pan with a bit of canola oil. Line the bottom of the pan with a round of parchment paper, and lightly grease the parchment paper.

In a small bowl, whisk together the flour, sugar, cocoa powder, and salt. In a medium bowl, beat the remaining ¼ cup oil and egg until combined. Add the food coloring and vanilla, and beat until well combined. Add the flour mixture and buttermilk alternately, beating on low speed after each addition just until combined. In a small bowl, stir together the vinegar and baking soda (mixture will foam), and fold into the batter. Spread batter into the prepared pan.

Bake until a toothpick comes out clean, 20 to 25 minutes. Cool the cake in pan on a wire rack for 10 minutes. Remove cake from pan; peel off and discard the parchment paper. Cool cake completely on a wire rack.

To make the frosting, in a large bowl, beat the shortening, cream cheese, and vanilla with an electric mixer on medium speed until light and fluffy, about 5 minutes. Gradually beat in powdered sugar to reach spreading consistency.

Spread the cake top and sides with about 1½ cups of the frosting. Spoon the remaining frosting into a decorating bag fitted with a 1M or 1B frosting tip. Pipe eight roses around the side of the cake.

COCKTAILS & DRINKS

SHE'S A PEACH

It's understandable that Mary, given George's sometimes surly attitude about life, might think he's not so keen on his brother Harry's new wife, Ruth, when he demonstrates little enthusiasm for the union. "Don't you like her?" she asks. "Well, of course I like her!" he says. "She's a peach!" This fruity white sangria is as sweet and refreshing as George is sour in that moment.

YIELD: 12 SERVINGS	ACTIVE: 10 MINUTES	TOTAL: 10 MINUTES + CHILLING

Two 750-ml bottles Albariño, Pinot Grigio, or Sauvignon Blanc

6 ounces peach brandy

4 ounces triple sec

2 cups orange juice

2 cups pineapple juice

2 medium ripe peaches, thinly sliced

2 lemons, thinly sliced

1 orange, thinly sliced

Ice

Divide the ingredients between two large pitchers or pour all into a large punch bowl. Stir to combine. Refrigerate at least 8 hours or up to 24 hours. Serve over ice.

MAMA AND PAPA DOLLAR

George and Mary loan out their own honeymoon savings to keep the Building and Loan in business, and they're left with just two dollars. "A toast! A toast to Mama Dollar and to Papa Dollar," George exclaims. "And if you want to keep this old Building and Loan in business, you better have a family real quick." These two dollar bills kept the Baileys in business, and in that same spirit, this recipe blends bourbon and brandy to create a tasty cocktail that's greater than the sum of its parts.

YIELD: 1 SERVING	ACTIVE: 5 MINUTES	TOTAL: 5 MINUTES

1 orange
1 ounce 80-proof bourbon
1 ounce 80-proof brandy
1 ounce sweet vermouth
2 dashes bitters
Ice

Use a citrus peeler to cut a thin piece of orange peel, about 4 inches long. Carefully coil the peel around a wooden skewer and hold in place for 10 seconds.

In a cocktail shaker, combine the bourbon, brandy, vermouth, and bitters. Add ice cubes; cover and shake until very cold. Strain into a rocks glass with a large ice ball or cube. Garnish with the orange twist.

HOMEMADE EGGNOG

No boxed product can hold a candle to the dreaminess of homemade eggnog. A custard is made with egg yolks, then chilled. Egg whites are beaten until frothy, then folded into the cold custard to create the experience of drinking a sweet, vanilla-and-nutmeg-flavored cloud.

YIELD: 6 SERVINGS	ACTIVE: 15 MINUTES	TOTAL: 15 MINUTES + CHILLING

4 egg yolks

⅓ cup plus 1 tablespoon sugar

2 cups whole milk

1 cup heavy cream

1 teaspoon freshly grated nutmeg

3 ounces bourbon

½ teaspoon vanilla extract

4 egg whites

In a large bowl, using a hand mixer or a stand mixer fitted with a whisk attachment, beat the egg yolks until they lighten in color. Gradually add ⅓ cup sugar, and beat until the sugar is completely dissolved.

In a medium saucepan over high heat, combine the milk, heavy cream, and nutmeg and bring to a boil, stirring occasionally. Remove from the heat, and gradually add to the sugar mixture, a little at a time, whisking constantly. Return the milk-egg mixture to the saucepan and cook over medium heat, whisking frequently, until the mixture reaches 160°F. Remove from the heat; stir in bourbon and vanilla. Pour into a medium bowl, and refrigerate until cold, about 2 hours.

In a large bowl, using a hand mixer or a stand mixer fitted with a whisk attachment, beat the egg whites until soft peaks form (tips curl). With the mixer running, gradually add the remaining 1 tablespoon sugar, and beat until stiff peaks form (tips stand straight). Carefully whisk the egg whites into the cold egg-milk mixture.

Serve immediately.

CLASSIC HOLIDAY PUNCH

A refreshing beverage served from a sparkling crystal bowl is essential for any holiday celebration. This bubbly libation of ginger ale, cranberry juice, and orange juice is festive and alcohol-free. If you'd like an adults-only version, swap the ginger ale for prosecco.

YIELD: 14 SERVINGS	ACTIVE: 15 MINUTES	TOTAL: 15 MINUTES + FREEZING

FOR THE ICE RING:

2 to 3 cups fresh cranberries, thin orange slices, and pomegranate arils

Fresh mint sprigs

1 cup club soda

1 to 2 cups cranberry juice

FOR THE PUNCH:

2 liters ginger ale, club soda, or sparkling water

2 cups orange juice or pineapple juice

4 cups cranberry juice

For the ice ring, place a 7- to 9-inch ring mold or 9- to 10-cup fluted cake pan in a pie plate (make sure the ring mold or pan fits inside the punch bowl). Place the cranberries, orange slices, pomegranate arils, and a few mint sprigs in the bottom of the ring mold or cake pan, filling about half full. In a pitcher, combine the club soda and cranberry juice. Carefully pour the cranberry mixture over the fruit to cover, leaving half an inch of space from the rim. Transfer the pie plate to a level space in the freezer. Let freeze for 8 hours or up to overnight.

Meanwhile, to make the punch, pour the ginger ale and juices into a punch bowl; stir to combine. Refrigerate until serving.

To remove the ice ring from the mold, place the bottom of the ring mold or cake pan in a large bowl of cold water for 2 to 3 minutes. Invert the mold or pan onto the cold pie plate, tapping on the bottom of the pan to release the ice ring. (If the ring doesn't release immediately, let it stand inverted for a few minutes.)

Pour the chilled punch into a large punch bowl. Add the ice ring.

ZUZU'S PETALS

Finding that Zuzu's petals are once again in his pocket helps George realize he's been given a second chance at life after a very dark journey through a world without him. Join George in a toast to the wonderfulness of life with this sparkling champagne-based drink flavored with Cointreau and rose syrup.

YIELD: 2 SERVINGS	ACTIVE: 5 MINUTES	TOTAL: 5 MINUTES

1 orange
1¼ ounces rose syrup
½ ounce Cointreau
Chilled champagne

Use a vegetable peeler to cut two long thin pieces of orange peel, each about 4 inches long. Carefully coil each peel around a wooden skewer, and hold in place for 10 seconds.

Divide the syrup and Cointreau among two champagne flutes. Fill the glasses with champagne, and hang an orange twist over the edge.

HOT RUM PUNCH

Clarence starts to order a flaming rum punch when he and George visit Nick's bar, the place that would have replaced Martini's if George had never been born, but he changes his mind in favor of a different drink. Clarence never gets it, but this hot rum punch is a good substitute, especially during the cold winter months.

YIELD: 12 SERVINGS	ACTIVE: 15 MINUTES	TOTAL: 15 MINUTES + STANDING

4 lemons
1 tangerine
¾ cup demerara sugar
4 cups boiling water
20 ounces amber rum
6 ounces cognac
Freshly grated nutmeg

Use a vegetable peeler to remove the peel from 2 of the lemons and the tangerine, avoiding the pith. In a medium bowl, combine the peels and sugar. Use the back of a spoon or a muddler to mix the sugar and peels. Cover and let stand for 2 hours or up to overnight.

Halve the tangerine and lemons, remove juice to equal ¾ cup, and add that to the sugar mixture.

Pour 1 cup of the boiling water over the sugar mixture, and stir until the sugar is dissolved. Transfer the sugar mixture to a punch bowl. Add the rum and cognac; stir to combine. Add the remaining 3 cups boiling water to the punch, and stir to combine.

Lightly grate nutmeg over punch, and ladle into glass cups.

MULLED WINE

Clarence orders two different drinks at Nick's bar, and he's clear about what he prefers in this spiced libation: Heavy on the cinnamon and light on the cloves (but not too light!). Though the owner of this hard-drinking joint didn't take too kindly to Clarence's request, you can enjoy this warming drink with friends in a more relaxed atmosphere than Nick's bar.

YIELD: 10 SERVINGS	ACTIVE: 10 MINUTES	TOTAL: 20 MINUTES

1 orange

1 lemon

10 whole cloves or allspice berries

4 peppercorns

4 star anise

Two 3-inch cinnamon sticks, plus more for serving

Two 750-ml bottles dry red wine

½ cup brandy

½ cup granulated sugar

Use a vegetable peeler to remove four long strips of orange peel and lemon peel. In a double-thick 6-inch square of cheesecloth, place the orange and lemon peels, cloves, peppercorns, star anise, and cinnamon sticks. Tie closed with cotton kitchen string.

Pour the wine, brandy, and sugar into a 4-quart saucepan; stir to combine. Add the spice bag, and bring the mixture to a boil over medium heat. Reduce the heat and simmer, covered, for 10 minutes. Remove and discard the spice bag.

Serve the mulled wine in cups with cinnamon sticks.

HOT COCOA

Sure to be a favorite among your little ones, this luscious hot cocoa is perfect for a cozy night in and guaranteed to get you into the holiday spirit!

YIELD: 4 SERVINGS	ACTIVE: 15 MINUTES	TOTAL: 15 MINUTES

⅓ cup unsweetened cocoa
  powder
¼ cup sugar
Pinch of salt
3 cups milk
½ teaspoon vanilla extract
9 large marshmallows

Combine the cocoa, sugar, and salt in a saucepan, and stir with a wooden spoon until well blended. Add a small amount of the milk, and stir to make a smooth paste, then stir in the remaining milk.

Cook the mixture over medium heat, stirring constantly, until tiny bubbles form around the edges of the pan, about 8 minutes. Do not boil.

Reduce the heat to low. Add the vanilla and 5 of the marshmallows. Cook, stirring constantly, until the marshmallows melt, about 5 minutes.

Ladle the hot chocolate into four mugs. Add a marshmallow to each mug, and serve immediately.

SPICED CIDER

This warming festive drink has a sweet and tart flavor.

YIELD: 12 SERVINGS	ACTIVE: 10 MINUTES	TOTAL: 30 MINUTES

1 gallon apple cider

¼ teaspoon ground cloves

3 cinnamon sticks, plus more for garnish

1 orange, sliced into wheels, plus more for garnish

½ teaspoon grated nutmeg

Bourbon (optional)

In a large saucepan, combine all the ingredients over medium heat. Bring the cider to a low simmer, then reduce heat to low and continue cooking for 20 minutes.

Strain the cider into mugs, and garnish with a cinnamon stick and an orange wheel perched on the rim. If desired, add 1 ounce bourbon to each mug.

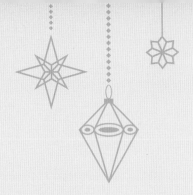

CHRISTMAS CRAFTS

EGG CARTON BELLS

As little Zuzu's teacher says, an angel gets their wings when you hear a bell ring. George, Mary, Zuzu, and all the Baileys can celebrate the promotions of their guardian angels with either of these easy-to-make bells, perfect for crafting with little ones.

SUPPLY LIST

- 2 paper egg cartons (each 12-space egg carton makes 6 to 8 bells)
- Scissors
- Non-toxic craft paint in desired colors
- Craft paintbrushes
- Glitter (optional)
- Clear spray sealant (optional)
- Wooden skewer
- 12 to 16 small jingle bells
- 12 to 16 pipe cleaners in desired colors
- Old newspaper or butcher paper
- Paper plates or cups

Adults should supervise children on this step: Cut each egg cup away from the carton, and note that not all cups will remain intact. Trim away any excess from the bottom rim, so each "bell" sits flat. You may want to add matching "notches" so the bell looks uniform all the way around.

Set out old newspaper to cover work surface. Pour a bit of each paint onto separate paper plates, and include a paintbrush with each color. If you plan on using them, set out the glitter shakers down the center of the workspace.

Paint and decorate the bells with your kids, friends, or family members, beginning with the insides of the bells, then outsides. You can use a different color for the inside of the bell, or match colors. While the outside of the bell is still wet with paint, sprinkle the glitter over the bell, if using. Set each bell aside to dry.

When the bells are completely dry, spray them with a coat of clear sealant, if you choose.

When the bells are decorated, dry, and sealed, use a sharp skewer to poke a hole through the top center of each bell.

Attach a jingle bell to the end of each pipe cleaner and twist to secure. Poke the pipe cleaner through the hole from the inside out. Create a hanger by using the extra pipe cleaner to form a loop, and secure with a twist.

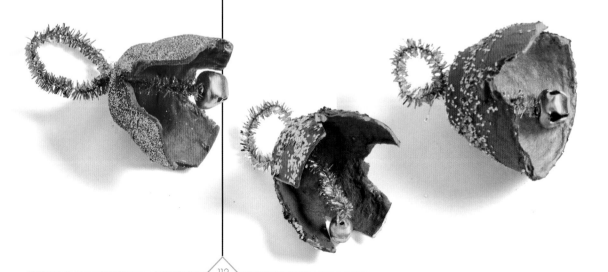

PAPER CUP BELLS

These bells are a bit more involved than the egg carton bells and are the perfect craft to do yourself or with older children. These instructions are enough for one set of bells, but you can make multiple sets to use as decorations throughout the house.

SUPPLY LIST

2 paper coffee cups

2 wooden skewers

Flower- and foam-safe spray paint, color of choice

1 pipe cleaner, color of choice

10 ½-inch bells

Two 1-inch bells

Washi tape (optional)

2 small beads with a hole big enough to thread the pipe cleaner through

Craft glue

Glitter glue (optional)

48 inches ribbon, colors of choice

Turn each coffee cup over so the bottom is facing up. Poke a hole in the center of each cup bottom with a skewer, leaving the skewer sticking out of the cup for now.

Using the skewer as a handle, spray paint the outside of the cup using multiple coats for total coverage. Allow to dry completely.

Thread five bells onto each pipe cleaner, rotating them so they fit snugly together. Finish with the large bell, and twist the end of the pipe cleaner to secure the cluster of bells.

If you choose, decorate the cups with washi tape as desired.

Thread the pipe cleaners into the cups, allowing the large bell to hang just below the rim of the cup. Thread the bead onto the pipe cleaner so it rests directly on the top of the bell (the bottom of the cup), and secure with a dot of glue. Allow to set.

Once the bead is set in place, form a large loop with the remaining length of pipe cleaner, and twist to secure. You may want to cover any visible glue with a ring of glitter glue around the base of the bead.

When the bells are ready to be hung, cut the ribbon in half creating two 24-inch lengths. Slip one pipe cleaner loop into the loop on the other bell, attaching the two bells together. Use one of the lengths of ribbon to tie a large bow around the base of the loops. Slip the remaining ribbon length through the exposed loop, and use it to hang the bells.

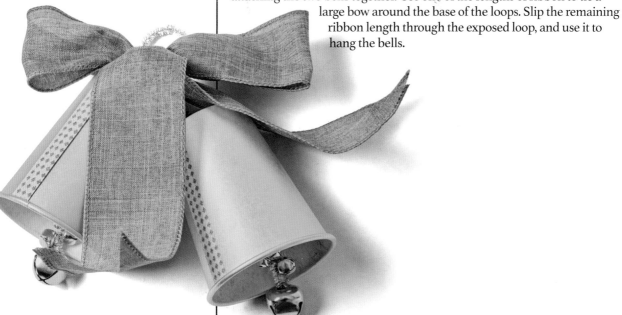

SALT DOUGH ORNAMENTS

Sure, you can buy ornaments to hang on your tree, but there's nothing like making keepsakes you'll remember forever. Mary Bailey and the kids make these salt dough ornaments in shapes that commemorate all the various ways the troops have found their way back from the war—ports, airports, roads, and more are filled with soldiers returning to their loved ones, and their loved ones welcoming them home.

SUPPLY LIST	

2 cups all-purpose flour (do not use self-rising), plus more for dusting

1 cup table salt

1 cup cold water

Food coloring (optional)

Cookie cutters

Jump ring

Non-toxic craft paint

Puff paint tubes (optional)

Paintbrushes

Clear spray sealant (optional)

Ribbon

In a large bowl, mix the flour and salt together, and then slowly add water, continuing to mix.

When the dough forms, turn out onto a lightly floured surface and knead for 5 minutes. You may color the dough with food coloring as desired by kneading it (wear gloves!) or by putting it in a plastic bag.

Chill the dough for at least 30 minutes.

When ready to roll out the dough, preheat the oven to 250°F. Have cookie sheets lined with parchment paper standing by. Roll the dough out on a floured surface to a scant ¼-inch thickness. Cut out desired shapes. Press a jump ring into the dough, burying the ring almost halfway, and leaving an edge outside. Keep in mind that later, you will loop ribbon through the edge that remains outside the dough.

Bake for 1 to 1½ hours or until completely dry and hard. Allow to cool completely.

Paint as desired. Puff paint is a fun way to add dimension to your ornaments.

Once the ornaments are decorated and complete, dry seal them with the spray sealant (if you choose to use it), and tie a ribbon through the jump ring for hanging.

CHRISTMAS CARD GARLAND

Where would any of us be without friends and family that live near and far, like Uncle Billy, Annie, Violet, or Sam Wainwright? Transform your holiday cards from years past into a garland with this family-friendly project that doubles as a keepsake.

SUPPLY LIST

Old Christmas cards and/or patterned card stock (this garland used about 24 Christmas cards and 3 pieces of 12-by-12-inch card stock)

1½-inch and 2½-inch craft punches (round, scallop, or plain)

Glue stick

2 large jars or vases (optional)

¼ inch ribbon (this garland used about 5 yards)

Fabric glue

Punch as many circles as possible from each card or piece of card stock, making an even number of each size. It will take six circles of the same size to make 1 sphere. This garland has sixteen large and eighteen small spheres.

Once all the circles have been cut, create stacks of six, arranging the colors and patterns as desired.

Work with one stack at a time. Take a circle from the top of the stack, and fold it exactly in half, patterned sides facing each other. Do the same for another circle from the same stack. Take the two folded circles, line up the edges of two sides (these should be the blank sides), and use the glue stick to glue them together. Repeat this process for the remaining circles in the stack, until all the circles have been incorporated into a sphere. Do not seal the last side. (You will seal the last side around ribbon later.) If you choose, place the sphere in the vases as you go, for safe keeping.

Repeat the gluing with your other stacks of circles, until spheres of both sizes have been made.

Working with the entire length of ribbon, measure your chosen lead (this garland has an 18-inch lead and tail). Choose a sphere, open it enough to fit the ribbon down inside as close to the center as possible, then seal it in with a thin line of fabric glue. Using a glue stick, glue together the final open sides of the sphere. Measure the desired spacing between spheres (this garland has approximately 3-inch spacing). Continue, with alternating sizes, until all the spheres are attached.

STRING BLOCK PRINTING

If you need decorations for your next holiday party, gather your little ones to help make gorgeous prints using nothing but string and wood blocks!

SUPPLY LIST

Scraps of wood or blocks (these will get paint on them)

Cotton kitchen twine

Old newspaper, for work surface

Craft or butcher paper

Paper plates, for paint palettes

Non-toxic craft paints

Wrap several blocks of wood with twine, creating different patterns. Keep some space between the strings to create crisp shapes.

Cover your work surface with old newspaper. Lay out craft paper for printing, and use a different paper plate for each paint color.

Start printing! Dab the block into the desired paint, and press against the paper. Allow the paint to dry completely before rolling up your paper and displaying it.

SCRAPPY FABRIC WREATHS

During Christmas, the Bailey Bros. Building & Loan office is cheerfully decorated with numerous fresh wreaths George has bought. But if you want a merry decoration that can be displayed all year long, these scrappy fabric wreaths are long-lasting and a beautiful craft to create with family members.

SUPPLY LIST

9 green fat quarters, a mix of light and dark

12-inch wire wreath form

9 small red ornaments, bells, pom-poms, or pine cones, as desired

3 pipe cleaners or florist wire

Find the long (21-inch) edge of each fat quarter. Measure 1½ inches away from the edge of the fabric, then use scissors to make a 2-inch cut into the long edge. Use this cut to tear straight down the fabric, creating a 1½-by-18-inch strip. Repeat until you have gone all the way across, creating about 14 strips.

Cut each strip in thirds, creating 1½-by-6-inch strips. Arrange the strips, alternating between light and dark fabrics.

Starting from the inner circle of the wire wreath form and working outward, fold each strip in half lengthwise around the wire form, wrong sides (the sides of fabric without the design) together, and tie a simple knot. As you continue adding fabric, push the knots tightly together to make each row as full as possible. Pull the strips to the front of the wreath, and form as necessary. Repeat with all rows in the form.

Once all the rows have been covered in fabric (you may have strips left over), fluff the strips, and pull any loose threads.

Use the pipe cleaners or wire to create "berry" clusters, and attach them to wreath. Attach ornaments, bells, pom-poms, or pine cones, as desired.

Hang using the form itself, or use an extra fabric strip to create a loop.

Note: If you want a less shaggy look, cut the fabric instead of tearing. A rotary cutter works well for this. If you buy yardage instead of fat quarters, purchase each fabric in half-yard pieces, and cut them in half, lengthwise. This wreath takes about 380 strips.

CHRISTMAS BOOK ANGEL

We've all got our guardians angels. Whether it's Clarence Odbody or any of your loved ones, those who look out for us should be celebrated at the holidays. These paper angels are an affordable way to bring an elegant Christmas touch to your home.

SUPPLY LIST

Box cutter or precision knife

A book between 250 and 500 pages (paperbacks work well)

Binder clips

Paper clips

Glue

2- to 2.5-inch wooden ball

Optional decorations: ribbon, glitter, pipe cleaner, sequins, flower- and foam-friendly spray paint.

Using the box cutter, remove the cover from the book, being careful to keep the spine intact. The more pages you have, the fuller the "gown" of the angel will be. However, more pages also make the project more complex. Once the cover is removed, you can choose to remove some pages from the book, if desired, by slicing a section away from the spine.

Once you have removed the cover and determined your desired page count for gown fullness, flex the pages open and closed around the spine a few times. Be sure to make bends at numerous points along the spine—this will help create the gown shape.

Find the middle of your book, splitting it in half as perfectly as possible. Then split each half in half again, as accurately as possible, to create fourths. Combine the two middle fourths and clip together. Mark the beginning of each side with a paper clip.

With the book lying flat in front of you (the center will be standing more or less upright), start with the top page on left side. Make your first fold by bringing the bottom left corner of the page up and in against the interior edge of the book (also known as the gutter). Make a sharp crease.

With that same page, make a second fold at the top left corner of the page, creating a point, then make another fold at the bottom right of the page near the gutter to create another point. Then complete the fold to create a crease that runs from the top left corner of the page to the bottom right corner of the page. This page will look like the beginnings of a paper airplane.

Using this folded page as 1, count back 10 pages, away from the center pages. On the tenth page, repeat fold one, bottom left corner to the gutter. For the second fold, bring the entire left edge (the left edge of the first fold) to the gutter. You should have a triangle that extends past the edges of the remaining pages.

Go back to the first (top) folded page, and find page 2 of the 10-page set. Repeat the folds, but extend the second fold a scant ¼ inch so a small point peeks out above the page. Continue folding pages 3 through 9, extending the second fold an additional ¼ inch each time to stagger the points. This creates the wings. When all 10 pages have been folded, use a large paper clip to hold the pages of the wing together. This will help keep it from getting damaged as you continue folding.

Now mirror these folds on the first 10 pages of the right-hand section, creating the second wing.

For all the remaining pages of the book, fold the top outer corner in to the gutter, and then make the same corner-to-corner "airplane" fold from earlier. It is important to keep the bottom edge corners very neat, because this creates the base of the angel's skirt and is a very visible part of the craft. Alternating from side to side and continuing to flex the spine will help create a more even gown.

Decorating the angel can be as simple as gluing a wooden ball or globe ornament on the top, creating a head.

For additional embellishments: The trim of the pictured gown was created by putting a plastic bag over the angels, leaving the desired trim width exposed and spray painting. Brush the wings lightly with glue, and then sprinkle with glitter. Glue small sequins on the gown. A pipe cleaner can be bent to create a halo and tucked into the back pages. Tie a bow at the neck.

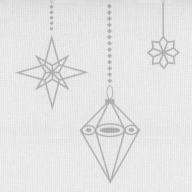

VINTAGE CHRISTMAS DINNER

There's nothing like celebrating the holidays with friends, family, or maybe even all of Bedford Falls. With these tips, you'll help your community have a day they'll remember for years to come.

HOW TO THROW THE PERFECT VINTAGE CHRISTMAS DINNER

There's nothing like celebrating the holidays with friends, family, or maybe even all of Bedford Falls. With these tips, you'll help your community have a day they'll remember for years to come.

HOSTING TIMELINE

3 TO 4 WEEKS AHEAD

Send out invitations: Make sure your guests have plenty of time to make arrangements to attend your event. Depending on where they are, and which holiday you're celebrating, you may want to send invitations as early as eight weeks ahead.

Plan the menu: With the recipes in this book, you'll have no shortage of menu options! By planning your meal well ahead of your event, you'll be able to keep an eye out for specials and deals. Additionally, think of which items, especially appetizers, can be made ahead, or if any dishes can be bought frozen. You'll also want to think about foods you may want to order ahead. Items to consider pre-ordering include turkeys, specialty cuts of meat, pies, or favorites wines. Lastly, always keep in mind your guests' dietary requirements or restrictions.

Prepare your event space: Make a list of action items to spruce up your house or event space—this will help you spread out chores and reduce stress. Your list might include freshening up outdoor plants, clearing up clutter, deep cleaning, or organizing the kitchen. You can also split up these responsibilities among members of your household. Final dusting and vacuuming should take place just before your event, but getting other chores done early will be a huge help.

Gather supplies: Do you have everything you need, and is it clean and ready to use? Think about seating, dinnerware, glassware, and serve ware. You don't want to find out at the last minute that all your wineglasses are dusty and you're missing some salad plates! Try borrowing supplies from friends and family before making plans to buy or rent them.

2 WEEKS AHEAD

Make your grocery list: Go through each dish on your menu, and create a shopping list. Sort by perishable and non-perishable items. Non-perishable items can be gathered at any time and kept aside until needed. Additionally, note which items must be purchased at specialty stores, so you can plan those trips accordingly.

Finalize your guest list: Hopefully, most guests have RSVP'd, but if you have a few stragglers, reach out to confirm their attendance.

1 WEEK AHEAD

Grocery list management: Do final shopping for non-perishables and drinks, and make sure that your list of perishables and last-minute items is up to date. Think about extra supplies you may need, such as ice, paper goods, and flowers.

5 DAYS AHEAD

Begin food preparation and safety check: When determining your cooking time, consider defrosting time, roasting time, and preheating time for foods such as turkey, ham, and other large cuts of meat. When thinking about dishes you can prepare ahead of time, check that you have the refrigerator space to store them. Perhaps a close friend or family member can lend you some space, if needed.

3 DAYS AHEAD

Make final assignments: Give each member of your household an index card with their responsibilities written on it. All final chores should be included, and even your youngest can help with simple chores, such as picking up toys or putting away extra coats and shoes. If friends or family outside of your household have offered to help, confirm their duties now.

Shop for perishables: Purchase the bulk of your groceries and flowers. Decide when last-minute items such as bread and baked goods will be picked up.

1 TO 2 DAYS AHEAD

Cleaning: Do the bulk of your vacuuming, dusting, and bathroom cleaning now, so that a last-minute touch-up will be quick.

Begin setting up: If possible, set up tables and chairs now.

Get ready to serve: Gather serving dishes, as well as slow cookers or chafing dishes. Put a sticky note on each serving piece with the name of its corresponding dish. Place a serving utensil nearby as well.

Begin cooking: Do any cooking, baking, or prepping that can be done in advance.

Schedule: Come up with a timeline for the day of the party. List when dishes must be cooked or reheated. Ask yourself when the final touches can be placed on tables, candles can be lit, and music started. Most importantly, think of when your household will get dressed in their party best.

DAY OF

Finally, the big day is here! Remember that even the best laid plans always have some problems. Get started early, so you can deal with any last-minute issues. Most importantly, enjoy the company of your loved ones, and remember that no one is a failure who has friends!

HOLIDAY DECORATING

VIGNETTES

Vignettes are a great way to display cherished items you've collected over the years that may not follow a collective theme. Think of each space where you will set out décor as a separate "stage." On each stage, create small scenes that tell a story.

COLLECTIONS

A grouping of similar items can make a big impact. A mantel full of snow globes or a tree covered in themed ornaments is a great way to show off your unique collection.

COLOR STORIES

Decorating with swaths of color is a beautiful way to create an effect. You may decide on an aesthetic such as monochrome or ombré. You can also rely on classic combos such as red and green, or silver and gold. Let the decorations you have on hand get you started, and augment if necessary.

VERTICAL SPACE

Tall vases and apothecary jars are a gorgeous and safe way to display vintage glass ornaments and other small décor without the risk of damage.

OUTDOOR DÉCOR

Yards, gardens, and porches can be used for more than just lights. Spruce up potted plants with cyclamen, pine cones, or evergreen clippings. Outdoor ornaments can be nestled among the plants. Decorate your mailbox or front entrance, if possible.

SETTING THE TABLE FOR A SIT-DOWN DINNER

As inviting as an ornately set table looks, it can be a difficult arrangement to pull off for larger parties. Opting for a simple family-style service allows for more time spent enjoying your guests. If young children are joining your table, offer small puzzles or coloring activities to help parents enjoy their meal as well. Older children and adults might enjoy conversation cards, trivia cards, or riddles. You may also choose to create place cards for your guests.

SIMPLE PLACE SETTINGS

Use only the plates and flatware required for the meal. Add extras, such as soup spoons or salad plates, only if the menu dictates. A water glass or an all-purpose glass is all that is needed at each place setting. Additionally, setting up a self-serve bar will let guests bring their own beverage to the table. This reduces table clutter.

FUNCTIONAL DÉCOR

A dramatic centerpiece looks great, and it can be fun to create, but it won't make a good dinner guest! If you are using a large arrangement, plan on relocating it just before guests sit down to dinner. A simpler choice is to use low décor, small vases, and votive candles that can easily shift as food is set down and guests begin eating. Incorporating items that are both festive and functional will add décor without creating extra clutter. Salt and pepper shakers, napkin folds, and name tags are just a few examples.

BUFFET SETUP

If you are hosting more guests than can comfortably sit at your table, having an open house, or just want a more casual atmosphere, serving food buffet-style is a great option.

GUEST FLOW

As previously mentioned, to prevent guests from gathering in one spot, use your whole space. Set up a bar away from the buffet table, and place appetizers away from the buffet table to help get guests mingling. When deciding the location of these stations, be mindful of any pets or young children.

DINING TABLE SETUP

Arrange plates and napkins, a few more than needed if possible. Use vases or tall sturdy glasses to hold the flatware. Cluster these items together at the start of your buffet table. You can also display flatware by wrapping each set in a napkin, securing with a ribbon, and placing in a low basket.

Arrange your empty platters on the table, making sure you have room for everything. Use cake stands, trifle bowls, or other taller vessels to take advantage of vertical space. Consider which items will need an electrical outlet, such as slow cookers or coffee urns. Arrange so that food items follow a progression, such as mains to sides, keeping garnishes or dressings next to the appropriate dishes.

You may want to label your dishes. If you have guests with dietary requirements, restrictions, or allergies, add place cards with the relevant information.

CLEAN UP

Place recycling containers and garbage bins in accessible locations to help your guests dispose of their own trash.

INDEX

**INSIGHT
EDITIONS**

PO Box 3088
San Rafael, CA 94912
www.insighteditions.com

f Find us on Facebook: www.facebook.com/InsightEditions
𝕐 Follow us on Twitter: @insighteditions

Library of Congress Cataloging-in-Publication Data available.

ISBN: 978-1-68383-945-3

INSIGHT EDITIONS
Publisher: Raoul Goff
VP of Licensing and Partnerships: Vanessa Lopez
VP of Creative: Chrissy Kwasnik
VP of Manufacturing: Alix Nicholaeff
Editorial Director: Vicki Jaeger
Designer: Judy Wiatrek Trum
Sponsoring Editors: Amanda Ng and Harrison Tunggal
Production Editor: Jennifer Bentham
Senior Production Manager: Greg Steffen
Senior Production Manager, Subsidiary Rights: Lina s Palma

Craft photography by Ben Hoedt and Ray Isaak Bleau.

Crafting directions and entertaining and decor ideas by
Elena P. Craig. A special thanks to her for recipe research
and inspiration.

WATERBURY PUBLICATIONS, INC.
Editorial Director: Lisa Kingsley
Creative Director: Ken Carlson
Associate Editor: Tricia Bergman
Associate Editor: Maggie Glisan
Associate Art Director: Doug Samuelson
Production Assistant: Mindy Samuelson
Photographer: Ken Carlson
Food Stylist: Jennifer Peterson
Food Stylist Assistant: Catherine Fitzpatrick

Insight Editions, in association with Roots of Peace, will plant two trees
for each tree used in the manufacturing of this book. Roots of Peace is
an internationally renowned humanitarian organization dedicated to
eradicating land mines worldwide and converting war-torn lands into
productive farms and wildlife habitats. Roots of Peace will plant two million
fruit and nut trees in Afghanistan and provide farmers there with the skills
and support necessary for sustainable land use.

Manufactured in China by Insight Editions

10 9 8 7 6 5 4 3 2 1